TOP **10**
PARIS

Top 10 Paris Highlights

Welcome to Paris............................**5**
Exploring Paris..............................**6**
Paris Highlights **10**
Musée du Louvre **12**
Musée d'Orsay **16**
Notre-Dame...................................**20**
Eiffel Tower...................................**24**
Sacré-Coeur...................................**26**
Arc de Triomphe **30**
Centre Georges Pompidou...........**32**
The Panthéon................................**34**
Sainte-Chapelle **36**
Hôtel des Invalides.......................**38**

The Top 10 of Everything

Moments in History.....................**42**
Historic Buildings........................**44**
Places of Worship **46**
Novels Set in Paris.......................**48**
Museums..**50**
Art Galleries **52**
Riverfront Sights **54**
Parks and Gardens.......................**56**
Off the Beaten Track.....................**58**
Children's Attractions..................**60**
Entertainment Venues.................**64**
Fine Dining **66**
Cafés and Bars..............................**68**
Shops and Markets.......................**70**
Paris for Free **72**
Festivals and Events....................**74**

CONTENTS

Paris
Area by Area

Ile de la Cité and Ile St-Louis **78**

Beaubourg and Les Halles..........**84**

Marais and the Bastille................**92**

Tuileries and Opéra Quarters....**102**

Champs-Elysées Quarter...........**110**

Invalides and
Eiffel Tower Quarters.............**118**

St-Germain, Latin and
Luxembourg Quarters **124**

Jardin des Plantes Quarter.......**134**

Chaillot Quarter.........................**140**

Montmartre and Pigalle **146**

Greater Paris...............................**154**

Streetsmart

Getting Around **164**

Practical Information.................**168**

Places to Stay.............................**172**

General Index **180**

Acknowledgments **188**

Phrase Book...............................**190**

Street Index **192**

Within each Top 10 list in this book, no hierarchy of quality or popularity is implied. All 10 are, in the editor's opinion, of roughly equal merit.

Title page, front cover and spine The elegant rotunda of Sacré-Coeur
Back cover, clockwise from top left Pretty outdoor tables in Montmartre; the ornate Hall of Mirrors in the Palace of Versailles; Apollo Fountain at Versailles; Eiffel Tower; Sacré-Coeur

The rapid rate at which the world is changing is constantly keeping the DK Eyewitness team on our toes. While we've worked hard to ensure that this edition of Paris is accurate and up-to-date, we know that opening hours alter, standards shift, prices fluctuate, places close and new ones pop up in their stead. So, if you notice we've got something wrong or left something out, we want to hear about it. Please get in touch at **travelguides@dk.com**

Welcome to
Paris

Paris, City of Light. Capital of romance and revolution. A heady mix of café philosophers and Coco Chanel couture. A foodie paradise. A culture-lover's dream. The focus of a thousand iconic movie images. Paris is all these things and more... so who could deny that it's Europe's most magical destination? With DK Eyewitness Top 10 Paris, it's yours to explore.

We love Paris: its culture, its charm, its *je ne sais quoi*. What could be better than exploring the chic shops of the **Marais** district or sniffing out the best cheeses in **Rue Montorgeuil**'s market; wandering through village-like **Montmartre** or browsing the bookstalls of the **Latin Quarter**; people-watching in the **Jardin du Luxembourg** or sauntering along **Boulevard St-Germain** for an early morning coffee at **Café de Flore** in the footsteps of Hemingway and Picasso? And what could be more fun than hopping on a Vélib' bike and cycling along the Seine from the **Eiffel Tower** to **Sainte-Chapelle**?

Paris is a city made for strolling, along its leafy boulevards and through its parks, against a backdrop of elegant Haussmann buildings and soaring contemporary structures. There's history in these cobblestoned streets, but Paris is also a striking 21st-century city, where cutting-edge art is displayed in the **Palais de Tokyo**, and a new generation of acclaimed chefs is experimenting and building upon Paris's reputation for gastronomic excellence.

Whether you're coming for a weekend or a week, our Top 10 guide brings together the best of everything that Paris has to offer, from the world-famous glories of the **Louvre** to the pretty lakes and waterfalls in **Bois de Vincennes**. The guide has useful tips through-out, from seeking out what's free to places off the beaten track, plus 11 easy-to-follow itineraries, designed to tie together a clutch of sights in a short space of time. Add inspiring photography and detailed maps, and you've got the essential pocket-sized travel companion. **Enjoy the book, and enjoy Paris.**

Clockwise from top: **Boulevard St-Germain, Sacré-Coeur, Versailles gardens, Centre Georges Pompidou, River Seine from Pont Alexandre III, Galeries Lafayette interior, Moulin Rouge**

Exploring Paris

Paris has an inexhaustible wealth of things to see and do. Here are some ideas for how to make the most of your time. The city is relatively compact, so you should be able to do most of your sightseeing on foot, and you're never far from a metro station.

Musée d'Orsay is housed in a former railway station.

Key
— Two-day itinerary
— Four-day itinerary

Two Days in Paris

Day ❶

MORNING

Cross **Pont Neuf** (see p80) over the River Seine to the Ile de la Cité and view the cathedral of **Notre-Dame** (see pp20–23), currently being restored after a fire in 2019, or visit **Sainte-Chapelle** (see pp36–7). Continue south into the lively **Latin Quarter** (see pp124–7) and pause for lunch in a Left Bank bistro (see p133).

AFTERNOON

Meander through the stylish district of **St-Germain-des-Prés** (see pp124–7) to the **Musée d'Orsay** (see pp16–19) and admire its impressive collection of Impressionist paintings. From here it's a short walk to **Hôtel des Invalides** (see pp38–9) and the **Eiffel Tower** (see pp24–5), stunningly lit up at night.

Day ❷

MORNING

Take in the views from atop the **Arc de Triomphe** (see pp30–31), then stroll the **Avenue des Champs-Elysées** (see p111) and **Jardin des Tuileries** (see p103) to the **Musée du Louvre** (see pp12–15).

AFTERNOON

Explore the hip **Marais** (see pp92–5), stopping at the **Centre Georges Pompidou** (see pp32–3). Rent a Vélib' bike and cycle to **Montmartre** (see pp146–9) and walk up to **Sacré-Coeur** (see pp26–7) for panoramic views.

Four Days in Paris

Day ❶

MORNING

Visit Montmartre's **Sacré-Coeur** (see pp26–7), then head down through

Panthéon's awe-inspiring interior features elegant arches, which link the pillars that support the dome.

Montmartre's leafy Place du Tertre, where artists set up their easels, is full of life and colour.

Pigalle *(see pp146–9)* to **Opéra National de Paris Garnier** *(see pp104–5)* and elegant **Place Vendôme** *(see p104)*.

AFTERNOON

Wander through **Jardin des Tuileries** *(see p103)* and visit Monet's *Water Lilies* at the **Musée de l'Orangerie** *(see p52)*. Then stroll along the **Avenue des Champs-Elysées** *(see p111)* to the **Arc de Triomphe** *(see pp30–31)*.

Day ❷

MORNING

Discover modern art at the **Centre Georges Pompidou** *(see pp32–3)*, then explore the fascinating **Musée Carnavalet** *(see p94)*. Enjoy a bistro lunch on **Place des Vosges** *(see p93)*.

AFTERNOON

See the **Marais** district *(see pp92–5)* and **Ile St-Louis** *(see pp78–81)*. Pass by **Notre-Dame** *(see pp20–23)* before enjoying **Sainte-Chapelle** *(see pp36–7)*.

Day ❸

MORNING

Take a boat trip along the River Seine *(see p170)* before a visit to the great Impressionists at the **Musée d'Orsay** *(see pp16–19)*.

AFTERNOON

Pay your respects to Napoleon at **Hôtel des Invalides** *(see pp38–9)* and then head to the **Eiffel Tower** *(see pp24–5)*.

Day ❹

MORNING

You'll have time to see all the star exhibits of the **Musée du Louvre** *(see pp12–15)* before heading off for lunch in the **Latin Quarter** *(see pp124–7)*.

AFTERNOON

Visit the **Panthéon** *(see pp34–5)*, explore the lovely **Jardin des Plantes** *(see p135)* and end the day strolling, and dining, around **Place de la Contrescarpe** *(see p136)*.

Top 10 Paris Highlights

Magnificent vaulting and stained-glass windows, Sainte-Chapelle

Paris Highlights	**10**	Arc de Triomphe	**30**
Musée du Louvre	**12**	Centre Georges Pompidou	**32**
Musée d'Orsay	**16**	The Panthéon	**34**
Notre-Dame	**20**	Sainte-Chapelle	**36**
Eiffel Tower	**24**	Hôtel des Invalides	**38**
Sacré-Coeur	**26**		

📏🔟 Paris Highlights

From Notre-Dame to the Eiffel Tower, Paris holds some of the world's most famous sights. These ten attractions should be top of the list for any first-time visitor, and remain eternally awe-inspiring.

Musée du Louvre ①

The world's most visited museum also contains one of the world's finest collections of art and antiquities (up to 1848). To complete the superlatives, it was once France's largest royal palace *(see pp12–15)*.

② Musée d'Orsay

This former railway station is one of the world's leading art galleries and, for many, reason alone to visit Paris *(see pp16–19)*.

Notre-Dame ③

This great Gothic cathedral, founded on the site of a Gallo-Roman temple, is a repository of art and history. It is also the geographical "heart" of France *(see pp20–23)*.

④ Eiffel Tower

More than seven million visitors a year ascend to the top of this famous Paris landmark for the spectacular views. It was erected for the Universal Exhibition of 1889 *(see pp24–5)*.

Sacré-Coeur ⑤

The terrace in front of this monumental white-domed basilica in Montmartre affords one of the finest free views over Paris *(see pp26–7)*.

6 Arc de Triomphe
Napoleon's triumphal arch, celebrating battle victories, stands proudly at the top of the Champs-Elysées and, along with the Eiffel Tower, is one of the city's most enduring images *(see pp30–31)*.

7 Centre Georges Pompidou
Home to France's National Museum of Modern Art, the building itself is a fascinating work of contemporary art *(see pp32–3)*.

Panthéon 8
The great and the good of France, including Voltaire, are buried in the Panthéon *(see pp34–5)*.

9 Sainte-Chapelle
Known as "a gateway to heaven", this exquisite church was built to house relics collected by St Louis on his Crusades *(see pp36–7)*.

10 Hôtel des Invalides
The glowing golden dome of the Hôtel des Invalides church is unmistakable across the rooftops of Paris. It houses Napoleon's tomb *(see pp38–9)*.

Musée du Louvre

One of the world's most impressive museums, the Louvre contains some 35,000 priceless objects. It was built as a fortress by King Philippe-Auguste in 1190, but Charles V (1364–80) made it his home. In the 16th century François I replaced it with a Renaissance-style palace and founded the royal art collection with 12 paintings from Italy. Revolutionaries opened the collection to the public in 1793. Shortly after, Napoleon renovated the Louvre as a museum.

1 Venus de Milo

This iconic statue of Greek goddess Aphrodite – later known as Venus by the ancient Romans – is the highlight of the museum's Greek antiques. It dates from the end of the 2nd century BCE and was discovered on the Greek island of Milos in 1820.

2 Marly Horses

Coustou's rearing horses **(above)** being restrained by horse-tamers were sculpted in 1745 for Louis XIV's Château de Marly. Replicas stand near the Place de la Concorde.

3 Mona Lisa

Arguably the most famous painting in the world, Leonardo da Vinci's portrait of a Florentine noblewoman with an enigmatic smile *(see p15)* has been beautifully restored. Visit early or late in the day.

4 Slaves

Michelangelo sculpted *Dying Slave* **(left)** and *Rebellious Slave* (1513–20) for the tomb of Pope Julius II in Rome. The unfinished figures seem to be emerging from their "prisons" of stone.

5 Glass Pyramid

The unmistakable glass and steel pyramid, designed by I M Pei, became the Louvre's new entrance in 1989. Stainless steel tubes make up the 21-m- (69-ft-) high frame.

6 Medieval Moats

An excavation in the 1980s uncovered the remains of the medieval fortress. You can see the base of the towers and the drawbridge support under the Cour Carrée.

7 The Winged Victory of Samothrace

This Hellenistic treasure (3rd–2nd century BCE) stands atop a stone ship radiating grace and power. It was created to commemorate a naval triumph at Rhodes.

8 The Raft of the Medusa

The shipwreck of a French frigate three years earlier inspired this gigantic early Romantic painting (left) by Théodore Géricault (1791–1824) in 1819. The work depicts the moment when the survivors spot a sail on the horizon.

9 Perrault's Colonnade

The majestic east façade by Claude Perrault (1613–88), with its paired Corinthian columns, was part of an extension plan commissioned by Louis XIV.

Musée du Louvre

- 10 The Lacemaker
- The Winged Victory of Samothrace 7
- The Raft of the Medusa 8
- Mona Lisa 3
- Marly Horses 2
- Dying Slave 4
- Perrault's Colonnade
- Glass Pyramid 5
- Venus de Milo 1
- Medieval Moats 6

Key
- Ground floor
- First floor
- Second floor

10 The Lacemaker

Jan Vermeer's masterpiece (above), painted around 1665, gives a simple but beautiful rendering of everyday life and is the highlight of the Louvre's Dutch collection.

Louvre Collections

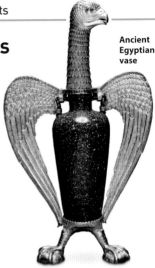

Ancient Egyptian vase

1 French Paintings
This superb collection ranges from the 14th century to 1848 and includes works by such artists as Jean Watteau, Georges de la Tour and J H Fragonard.

2 French Sculpture
Highlights include the Tomb of Philippe Pot by Antoine le Moiturier, the Marly Horses *(see p12)* and works by Pierre Puget.

3 Egyptian Antiquities
The finest collection outside Cairo, featuring a Sphinx in the crypt, the Seated Scribe of Sakkara, huge sarcophagi, mummified animals, funerary objects and intricate carvings depicting life in Ancient Egypt.

4 Greek Antiquities
The art of Ancient Greece here ranges from a Cycladic idol from the third millennium BCE to Classical Greek marble statues (c.5th century BCE) to Hellenistic works (late 3rd–2nd century BCE).

Louvre Collections

Key
Basement
Ground floor
First floor
Second floor

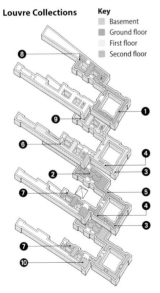

5 Near Eastern Antiquities
This stunning collection includes a recreated temple of an Assyrian king and the Codex of Hammurabi (18th-century BCE), mankind's oldest written laws.

6 Italian Paintings
French royalty adored the art of Italy and amassed much of this collection (1200–1800). It includes many works by Leonardo da Vinci.

7 Italian Sculpture
Highlights of this collection, dating from the early Renaissance, include a 15th-century *Madonna and Child* by Donatello and Michelangelo's *Slaves (see p12)*.

8 Dutch Paintings
Rembrandt's works are hung alongside domestic scenes by Vermeer and portraits by Frans Hals.

9 Objets d'Art
The ceramics, jewellery and other items in this collection encompass swathes of history.

10 Islamic Art
This exquisite collection, which spans 13 centuries and 3 continents, is covered by an ultra-modern glass veil.

LEONARDO DA VINCI AND THE MONA LISA

Leonardo da Vinci, Renaissance man extraordinaire, was not only an artist but also a sculptor, engineer, architect and scientist. His many interests included the study of anatomy and aerodynamics.

Born in Vinci to a wealthy family, Leonardo da Vinci (1452–1519) took up an apprenticeship under Florentine artist Andrea del Verrocchio, then served the Duke of Milan as an architect and military engineer, during which time he painted the *Last Supper* mural (1495). On his return to Florence, to work as architect to Cesare Borgia, he painted his most celebrated portrait, the *Mona Lisa* (1503–06). It is also known as *La Gioconda*, allegedly the name of the model's aristocratic husband, although there is ongoing speculation regarding the identity of the subject. The work, in particular the sitter's mysterious smile, shows mastery of two techniques: *chiaroscuro*, the contrast of light and shadow, and *sfumato*, subtle transitions between colours. It was the artist's own favourite painting and he took it with him everywhere. In 1516 François I brought them both to France, giving da Vinci the use of a manor house in Amboise in the Loire Valley, where he died three years later.

Mona Lisa, da Vinci's enigmatic portrait

TOP 10 ARCHAEOLOGICAL TREASURES

1 Hammurabi's Code (1792–1750 BCE)

2 Parthenon Marbles (5–4th century BCE)

3 Assyrian Lamussa (713 BCE)

4 Ain Ghazal Statue (7000 BCE)

5 Chapel to Tomb of Akhethotep (2400 BCE)

6 The Monzon Lion (12–13th century)

7 The Louvre Doll (3rd–4th century)

8 Frieze of Lions (510 BCE)

9 Bull's head column capital (510 BCE)

10 The Seated Scribe (2600–2500 BCE)

Musée d'Orsay

This world-class collection covers a variety of art forms from the years 1848 to 1914, and includes a superb Impressionist section. Its setting, in a converted railway station, is equally impressive. Built in 1900, in time for the Paris Exposition, the station was in use until 1939, when it was closed and largely ignored, although it was the location for Orson Welles' 1962 film, The Trial. It was later used as a theatre and as auction rooms, and in the mid-1970s was considered for demolition. In 1977, the Paris authorities decided to save the defunct station building by converting it into this striking museum.

3 The Building

The former railway station that houses this museum (left) is almost as stunning as the exhibits. The light and spacious feel on stepping inside, after admiring the magnificent old façade, takes one's breath away.

Van Gogh Paintings 4

The star of the collection is Vincent van Gogh (1853–90) and the most striking of the canvases on display is the 1889 work showing the artist's Bedroom at Arles (right). Also on display are some of the artist's self-portraits, painted with his familiar intensity.

1 Le Déjeuner sur l'Herbe

Edouard Manet's (1832–83) controversial painting (1863) was first shown in an "Exhibition of Rejected Works". Its bold portrayal of a classically nude woman enjoying the company of 19th-century men in suits brought about a wave of criticism.

6 Degas' Statues of Dancers

The museum has a exceptional collection of works by Edgar Degas (1834–1917). Focusing on dancers (left) and the world of opera, his sculptures range from innocent to erotic. Young Dancer of Fourteen (1881) was the only one exhibited in the artist's lifetime.

2 A Burial at Ornans

This canvas depicting a sombre provincial funeral was painted by Gustave Courbet (1819–77) in 1849. Scorned by the establishment of the day, it is now seen as a landmark in French realist painting.

5 Blue Waterlilies

Claude Monet (1840–1926) painted this stunning canvas (1919) on one of his favourite themes. His love of waterlilies led him to create his own garden at Giverny in order to paint them in a natural setting. This work inspired many abstract painters later in the 20th century.

7 Jane Avril Dancing

Toulouse-Lautrec's (1864–1901) paintings define Paris's *belle époque*. Jane Avril was a famous Moulin Rouge dancer and featured in several of his works, like this 1895 canvas **(left)**, which Toulouse-Lautrec drew from life, in situ at the cabaret.

8 Dancing at the Moulin de la Galette

One of the best-known paintings of the Impressionist era (1876), this work was shown at the Impressionist exhibition in 1877. The exuberance of Renoir's (1841–1919) work captures the look and mood of Montmartre and is one of the artist's masterpieces.

9 La Belle Angèle

This portrait of a Brittany beauty (1889) by Paul Gauguin (1848–1903) shows the influence of Japanese art on the artist. It was bought by Degas, to finance Gauguin's first trip to Polynesia.

10 Café Campana

Offering a rest from all the impressive art, the museum's café, renovated by the Campana Brothers, is delightfully situated behind one of the former station's huge clocks. A break here is an experience in itself and the food is good too.

NEED TO KNOW

MAP J2 ■ Esplanade Valéry Giscard d'Estaing 75007 ■ 01 40 49 48 14 ■ www.musee-orsay.fr

Open 9:30am–6pm Tue–Sun (to 9:45pm Thu); closed 1 May & 25 Dec

Adm €16 (under-18s free, under-26s EU only free); free first Sun of month; pre-booking a timed entry slot online is advisable, even for visitors who benefit from free entry

■ Café Campana, situated on the fifth floor, is open for lunch, snacks and drinks from Tuesdays through Sundays, plus dinner on Thursdays.

■ Music concerts are often held. Concert tickets include free museum entry.

Museum Guide
It's best to pick up a floorplan as soon as you enter the gallery to find out where the works or collections you want to see are on display. In general, the upper level is home to the Impressionist and Post-Impressionist galleries, while the ground floor has works from the Academic, Realist and Symbolist movements. Decorative arts from the 1900s, including a fine Art Nouveau collection, are in the Pavillon Amont, on the ground floor as well as on floors 2, 3 and 4. The ground floor has a bookshop and a gift store.

Musée d'Orsay Collections

1 The Impressionists
One of the best Impressionist collections in the world. Admirers of Manet, Monet and Renoir will not be disappointed.

2 The Post-Impressionists
The artists who moved on to a newer interpretation of Impressionism are equally well represented, including Matisse, Toulouse-Lautrec and the towering figure of Van Gogh.

3 School of Pont-Aven
Paul Gauguin was at the centre of the group of artists associated with Pont-Aven in Brittany. His work here includes *Yellow Haystacks*, painted when the artist visited the region in 1889.

4 Art Nouveau
Art Nouveau is synonymous with Paris, with many metro stations retaining entrances built in that style. Pendants and glassware by René Lalique (1860–1945) are among the examples on display here.

5 Symbolism
This vast collection includes works by well-known artists such as Gustav Klimt (1862–1918) and Edvard

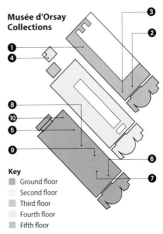

Musée d'Orsay Collections

Key
- Ground floor
- Second floor
- Third floor
- Fourth floor
- Fifth floor

Munch (1863–1944), and James Whistler's (1834–1903) portrait of his mother, dating from 1871.

6 Romanticism
The Romantics wanted to raise awareness about the spiritual world. One fine example is *The Tiger Hunt* (1854) by Eugène Delacroix (1798–1863).

7 Sculpture
The collection includes pieces by Rodin *(see p120)* and satirical carvings of politicians by Honoré Daumier (1808–79).

8 Naturalism
Naturalist painters intensified nature in their work. *Haymaking* (1877) by Jules Bastien-Lepage (1848–84) is a fine example.

9 Nabis
The Nabis Movement made art into a more decorative form. Pierre Bonnard (1867–1947) is one of its founding members.

10 Architecture
In addition to the 19th-century architectural etchings and drawings, there is a room dedicated to the creation of the Opéra Garnier *(see p104)*.

Blue Dancers (1890), **Edgar Degas**

THE IMPRESSIONIST MOVEMENT

Regarded as the starting point of modern art, the Impressionist Movement is the best-known and best-loved art movement in the world – certainly if the popularity of the Musée d'Orsay is anything to go by. It began in France, and almost all its leading figures were French. Impressionism was a reaction against the formality and Classicism insisted upon by the Académie des Beaux-Arts in Paris, which was very much the art establishment, deciding what would or would not be exhibited at the Paris Salon. The term "impressionism" was coined by a critic of the style, who dismissed the 1872 Monet painting *Impression: Sunrise*,

now on display at the Musée Marmottan (*see p157*). The artists themselves then adopted the term. The style influenced Van Gogh and was to have a lasting influence on 19th- and 20th-century art.

Cathedral at Rouen
(1892–3), Claude Monet

TOP 10 IMPRESSIONISTS

1 Claude Monet
(1840–1926)

2 Edouard Manet
(1832–83)

3 Auguste Renoir
(1841–1919)

4 Edgar Degas
(1834–1917)

5 Camille Pissarro
(1830–1903)

6 Alfred Sisley
(1839–99)

7 James Whistler
(1834–1903)

8 Walter Sickert
(1860–1942)

9 Mary Cassatt
(1844–1926)

10 Berthe Morisot
(1841–95)

On the Beach (1873), Edouard Manet

TOP 10 ★ Notre-Dame

The "heart" of the country, both geographically and spiritually, the Cathedral of Notre-Dame (Our Lady) stands on the Ile de la Cité. After Pope Alexander III laid the foundation stone in 1163, an army of craftsmen toiled for 170 years to realize Bishop Maurice de Sully's magnificent design. Almost destroyed during the Revolution, the Gothic masterpiece was restored in 1841–64 by architect Viollet-le-Duc. The wooden spire was destroyed by fire in 2019. A restoration programme is underway, due to be completed in 2024.

1 Portal of the Last Judgment

This central relief over the doors of Notre-Dame depicts the biblical Last Judgment – when the souls of humankind will stand before God. The good souls move to the right, towards paradise, while the souls of the condemned move to the left and are led to hell. Though completely damaged during the Revolution, the portal was restored brilliantly in the 19th century.

2 Point Zero

Roads in France are measured from this plaque in front of the church, making it the very center of the whole country – technically. Legend has it that any visitor who steps on it will inevitably return to Paris one day.

3 Portal of the Virgin

The splendid stone tympanum (right) was carved in the 13th century and shows the Virgin Mary's death and coronation in heaven. However, the statue of the Virgin and Child that stands between the doors is a modern replica.

4 Flying Buttresses

The flying buttresses supporting the cathedral's east façade are by architect Jean Ravy. The best view is from Square Jean XXIII.

5 West Front

The entrance to the cathedral (right) is through three elaborately carved portals. Biblical scenes, sculpted in the Middle Ages, depict the Life of the Virgin, the Last Judgment and the Life of St Anne.

6 Gallery of Kings

The west façade of Notre-Dame cathedral is adorned with the statues of the kings from the book of Judah. During the French Revolution the heads of these statues were chopped off, symbolically believed to be the kings of France. The missing heads were found nearly 200 years later at a construction site nearby and are now on display.

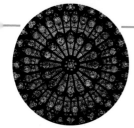

7 Rose Windows

Three great rose windows adorn the north, south and west façades, but only the north window **(left)** retains its 13th-century stained glass, depicting the Virgin surrounded by figures from the Old Testament. The south window shows Christ encircled by the Apostles.

8 Gargoyles

A key feature of the Gothic style of architecture, these grotesque statues stretch from the cathedral's roof and channel water off the roof, acting as waterspouts. On a rainy day, visitors can see the water pouring from their mouths.

9 Galerie des Chimères

Lurking behind the upper gallery between the towers are decorative sculptures or *chimères* **(above)**, placed here to ward off evil.

10 The Towers

The Gothic towers are 69 m (226 ft) high; 387 steps within the north tower lead to great views. The south tower houses the Emmanuel Bell, forged in 1685 and rung on special occasions.

NEED TO KNOW

MAP N4 ■ 6 Parvis Notre-Dame – Pl Jean-Paul II, 75004 ■ 01 53 10 07 00 (towers); 01 42 34 56 10 (cathedral) ■ www.notredamedeparis.fr

The cathedral is currently closed to the public due to ongoing restoration work.

The Fire of Notre-Dame
On 15 April 2019, fire broke out near the cathedral's spire during renovation work. Watched by many onlookers, the fire quickly spread to the east and west along the roof, which was partially covered in scaffolding at the time. As the flames reached the Gothic towers, the spire collapsed and crashed through the vaulted roof. It took 500 firefighters more than 12 hours to extinguish the inferno. It is thought the cathedral was 30 minutes away from being all but destroyed had the fire engulfed the bell towers, causing them to fall. Many of the priceless treasures and artworks were rescued from the blaze; the 16 copper roof statues had already been removed due to the refurbishment. The vaulted stone ceiling and the cathedral's rose windows mostly survived. The government has set an ambitious goal to have the cathedral restored to its former glory by 2024 – including, after much public debate, a faithful reconstruction of the original spire.

Famous Visitors to Notre-Dame

1 Joan of Arc
The patriot Jeanne d'Arc (1412–31), who defended France against the invading English, had a posthumous trial here in 1455, despite having been burned at the stake 24 years earlier. She was found to be innocent of heresy.

2 François II and Mary Stuart
Mary Stuart (Mary Queen of Scots; 1542–87) had been raised in France and married the Dauphin in 1558. He ascended the throne as François II in 1559 and the king and queen were crowned in Notre-Dame.

3 Napoleon
The coronation of Napoleon (1769–1821) in Notre-Dame in 1804 saw the eager general seize the crown from Pope Pius VII and crown himself emperor and his wife, Josephine, empress.

Statue of Joan of Arc inside Notre-Dame

4 Josephine
Josephine's (1763–1814) reign as Empress of France lasted only five years; Napoleon divorced her in 1809.

5 Pope Pius VII
In 1809 Pope Pius VII (1742–1823), who oversaw Napoleon's Notre-Dame coronation, was taken captive when the emperor declared the Papal States to be part of France. The pope was imprisoned at Fontainebleau, 50 km (30 miles) south of Paris.

6 Philip the Fair
In 1302 the first States General parliament was formally opened at Notre-Dame by Philip IV (1268–1314), otherwise known as Philip the Fair. He greatly increased the governing power of the French royalty.

7 Henry VI of England
Henry VI (1421–71) became King of England at the age of one. Like his father, Henry V, he also claimed France and was crowned in Notre-Dame in 1430.

8 Marguerite of Valois
In August 1572, Marguerite (1553–1589), sister of Charles IX, stood in the Notre-Dame chancel during her marriage to the Protestant Henri of Navarre (1553–1610), while he stood alone by the door.

9 Henri of Navarre
As a Protestant Huguenot, Henri's marriage to the Catholic Marguerite resulted in uprising and many massacres. In 1589, he became Henri IV, the first Bourbon king of France, and converted to Catholicism, stating that "Paris is well worth a Mass".

10 Charles de Gaulle
On 26 August 1944, Charles de Gaulle entered Paris and attended a Magnificat service to celebrate the liberation of Paris, despite the fact that hostile snipers were still at large outside the cathedral.

Charles de Gaulle visits Notre-Dame

SAVING NOTRE-DAME

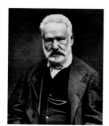

Novelist Victor Hugo

Paris's great cathedral has had a history of deterioration and restoration. When Victor Hugo's novel *Notre-Dame de Paris (The Hunchback of Notre-Dame)* was published in 1831, the cathedral was in a state of decay. Even for the crowning of Napoleon in 1804, the crumbling setting had to be disguised with ornamentation. During the Revolution, the cathedral was sold to a scrap dealer, though fortunately not demolished. Hugo was intent on saving France's spiritual heart and helped mount a campaign to restore Notre-Dame before it was too late; Eugène Emmanuel Viollet-le-Duc (1814–79) was chosen for the restoration. Repairs began again in 2019 before the cathedral was damaged by fire. Within 24 hours of the blaze, President Macron vowed to rebuild Notre-Dame and more than €800 million was raised. At the same time, sales of Hugo's iconic novel rocketed, prompting French booksellers to ask for profits from renewed sales to be directed towards the restoration.

TOP 10
EVENTS IN NOTRE-DAME HISTORY

1 Construction of the cathedral begins (1163)

2 St Louis places the Crown of Thorns here temporarily (1239)

3 Construction is completed (1334)

4 Retrial of Joan of Arc (1455)

5 Revolutionaries loot the cathedral and make it a Temple of Reason (1789)

6 Crowning of Emperor Napoleon (1804)

7 Restoration work is completed (1864)

8 Mass for the Liberation of Paris (1944)

9 New bells with a medieval tone mark the 850th anniversary (2013)

10 Fire destroys the spire and roof (2019)

The Hunchback of Notre-Dame, Hugo's 1831 novel, tells the story of Quasimodo, a hunchbacked bell-ringer at Notre-Dame, who falls in love with gypsy girl Esmeralda.

TOP10 ⭐ Eiffel Tower

The most distinctive symbol of Paris, the Eiffel Tower was much maligned by critics when it appeared on the city's skyline in 1889 as part of the Universal Exhibition, but its graceful symmetry soon made it the star attraction. A feat of engineering, at 324 m (1,062 ft) high, it was the world's tallest building until it was surpassed by New York's Chrysler Building in 1930. Despite its delicate appearance, it weighs 10,100 metric tons and engineer Gustave Eiffel's construction was so sound that it never sways more than 7 cm (2.5 in) in strong winds.

The iconic Eiffel Tower

3 Lighting
Some 20,000 bulbs and 336 lamps make the Eiffel Tower **(left)** a spectacular night-time sight. It sparkles like a giant Christmas tree for five minutes every hour from dusk until 1am.

4 View from the Trocadéro
Day or night, the best approach for a first-time view of the tower is from the Trocadéro *(see p142)*, which affords a monumental vista from the Chaillot terrace across the Seine.

1 Gustave Eiffel's Office
Located at the top of the tower is Gustave Eiffel's office, which has been restored to its original condition. It displays wax models of Thomas Edison and Eiffel himself.

2 First Level
You can walk the 345 steps up to the 57-m- (187-ft-) high first level and enjoy a hearty meal at the all-day brasserie. This level also includes glass floors and educational displays.

5 Viewing Gallery
At 276 m (906 ft), the stupendous view **(right)** stretches for 80 km (50 miles) on a clear day. You can also see Gustave Eiffel's sitting room on this level.

7 **Champ-de-Mars**
The long gardens of this former parade ground stretch from the base of the tower to the École Militaire (military school).

8 **Ironwork**
The complex pattern of the girders **(above)**, held together by 2.5 million rivets, stabilizes the tower in high winds. The metal can expand up to 15 cm (6 in) on hot days.

9 **Hydraulic Lift Mechanism**
The 1899 lift mechanism is still in operation and travels some 103,000 km (64,000 miles) a year. The uniformed guard clinging to the outside is a model.

10 **Bust of Gustave Eiffel**
This bust of the tower's creator **(below)**, by Antoine Bourdelle, was placed below his achievement, by the north pillar, in 1929.

6 **Second Level**
At 116 m (380 ft) high, this level is the location of Le Jules Verne restaurant, one of the finest in Paris for food and views (see p123). It is reached by a private lift in the south pillar.

THE LIFE OF GUSTAVE EIFFEL

Born in Dijon, Gustave Eiffel (1832–1923) was an engineer and builder who made his name building bridges and viaducts, and helped in the design of the Statue of Liberty. Eiffel was famous for the graceful designs and master craftsmanship of his many wrought-iron constructions. He once said that his famous tower was "formed by the wind itself". In 1890 he became immersed in the study of aerodynamics, and kept an office in the tower until his death, using it for experiments. In 1889, when the Eiffel Tower was erected, its creator was awarded the Légion d'Honneur.

NEED TO KNOW

MAP B4 ■ Champ de Mars, 7e ■ 08 92 70 12 39 ■ www.toureiffel.paris

Open Generally 9:30am–11.45pm (last adm 10.45pm) daily, but check online for the latest times; stairs sometimes close at 6pm. Closed 14 Jul.

For elevator access to the top €26.80; €13.40 for 12–24 yr olds; €6.70 under 12s.

■ There are restaurants and snack bars on levels 1 and 2, along with a Champagne bar on level 3, plus a variety of food kiosks around the tower's base.

■ Skip the queue and book your ticket online or opt for a guided tour (cultival.fr).

TOP10 ⭐ Sacré-Coeur

One of the city's most photographed sights, the spectacular white basilica of Sacré-Coeur (Sacred Heart) watches over Paris from its highest point. The basilica was built as a memorial to the 58,000 French soldiers killed during the Franco-Prussian War (1870–71). It took 46 years to build and was finally completed in 1923 at a cost of 40 million francs (6 million euros). Priests still pray for the souls of the dead here, 24 hours a day, as they have since 1885. People flock here for the breathtaking panoramic views – at sunset, in particular, there are few sights in Paris more memorable.

1 Great Mosaic of Christ

A glittering Byzantine mosaic of Christ, created by Luc Olivier Merson between 1912 and 1922, decorates the vault over the chancel. It represents France's devotion to the Sacred Heart.

3 Bronze Doors

The doors of the portico entrance are beautifully decorated with bronze relief sculptures depicting the Last Supper and other scenes from the life of Christ.

4 The Dome

The distinctive egg-shaped dome of the basilica is the second-highest view-point in Paris after the Eiffel Tower. Reached via a spiral staircase, vistas can stretch as far as 48 km (30 miles) on a clear day.

5 Statue of Christ

The basilica's most important statue shows Christ giving a blessing. It is sym-bolically placed in a niche over the main entrance, above the two bronze eques-trian statues.

2 Crypt Vaults

The arched vaults of the crypt (above) house a chapel that contains the heart of Alexandre Legentil, one of the advocates of Sacré-Coeur.

6 Stained-Glass Gallery

One level of the great dome is encircled by stained-glass windows **(right)**. From here there is a beautiful view over the whole interior.

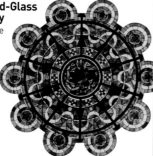

7 Bell Tower

The *campanile*, designed by Lucien Magne and added in 1904, is 80 m (262 ft) high. One of the heaviest bells in the world, the 19-ton La Savoyarde hangs in the belfry. Cast in Annecy in 1895, it was donated by the dioceses of Savoy.

8 Façade

Architect Paul Abadie (1812–1884) employed a mix of domes, turrets and Classical features in his design of this basilica. The Château-Landon stone secretes calcite when wet and so it keeps the façade **(left)** bleached white.

THE FRANCO-PRUSSIAN WAR

In 1870, as Prussia made moves to take over the rest of Germany, France was also threatened by its military power. France declared war on Prussia in July, but the country was ill-prepared and in September Napoleon III was captured. Parisians held fast, defending their city with homemade weapons. But by January 1871 they surrendered. Two Catholic businessmen made a vow in 1870 to build a church dedicated to the Sacred Heart of Jesus as penance as they felt that France's misfortune had a spiritual cause.

10 Equestrian Statues

Two striking bronze statues of French saints stand on the portico above the main entrance, cast in 1927 by Hippolyte Lefèbvre. One statue is of Joan of Arc, while the other is of Louis IX, who was later canonized as Saint Louis.

9 The Funicular

To avoid the steep climb up to Sacré-Coeur, take the *funiculaire* cable railway **(below)**; access is with a standard metro ticket. It runs from the end of rue Foyatier, by Square Willette.

NEED TO KNOW

MAP F1 ■ 35 Rue du Chevalier-de-la-Barre, 75018 ■ 01 53 41 89 00 ■ www.sacre-coeur-montmartre.com

Basilica: open 6am–10:30pm daily, last entry 10:15pm

Dome: open Oct–Feb: 10:30am–5:30pm daily; Mar–May: 10:30am–7pm daily; Jun–Sep: 10:30am–8:30pm daily; adm €8

■ Grab a bite at Le Refuge, 72 rue Lamarck and watch the world go by.

■ A sung Mass takes place on Sundays at 11am.

Following pages Arc de Triomphe illuminated at dusk

Arc de Triomphe

Flush from his victory at Austerlitz in 1805, Napoleon commissioned the Arc de Triomphe as a tribute to his Grande Armee. Although construction began on the 50-m (164-ft) arch in 1806, it was not completed until 1836, a long delay that was due, in part, to Napoleon's fall from power. Four years later, his funeral procession passed beneath it, on its way to his burial in Les Invalides. All traffic is banned along the Champs-Elysées on the first Sunday of every month, making it easier to access and get that perfect photo of the beautiful Arc de Triomphe.

4 Tomb of the Unknown Soldier

In the centre of the arch flickers the eternal flame on the Tomb of the Unknown Soldier **(left)**, a victim of World War I buried on 11 November 1920. It is symbolically reignited every day at 6:30pm.

1 Museum

Within the arch is a small but interesting museum which tells the history of its construction and gives details of various celebrations and funerals that the arch has seen over the years. The more recent of these are shown in a short video.

2 Departure of the Volunteers in 1792

One of the most striking sculptures is on the front right base. It shows French citizens leaving to defend their nation against Austria and Prussia.

3 Triumph of Napoleon

As you look at the arch from the Champs-Elysées (see p111), J P Cortot's high-relief on the left base shows the restored *Triumph of Napoleon*. It celebrates the Treaty of Vienna peace agreement signed in 1810, when Napoleon's empire was in its heyday.

5 Viewing Platform

Take the elevator or climb 284 steps to the top of the Arc de Triomphe to get a sublime view **(below)** of Paris and a sense of the arch's dominant position in the centre of the Place de l'Etoile. To the east is the Champs-Elysées and to the west is the Grande Arche de La Défense (see p155). There are another 40 steps after the lift.

Arc de Triomphe

6 Battle of Aboukir

Above the *Triumph of Napoleon* carving is this scene **(above)** showing Napoleonic victory over the Turks in 1799. The same victory was commemorated on canvas in 1806 by the French painter Antoine Gros and is now on display at the Palace of Versailles *(see p155)*.

7 Battle of Austerlitz

Another battle victory is shown on a frieze on the arch's north side. It depicts Napoleon's heavily outnumbered troops breaking the ice on Lake Satschan in Austria, a tactic which drowned thousands of enemy troops.

8 Frieze

A frieze running around the arch shows French troops departing for battle (east) and their victorious return (west).

THE GREAT AXIS

The Arc de Triomphe is the central of three arches; together they create a grand vision of which even Napoleon would have been proud. He was responsible for the first two, placing the Arc de Triomphe directly in line with the Arc de Triomphe du Carrousel in front of the Louvre *(see pp12–15)*, which also celebrates the victory at Austerlitz. In 1989, the trio was completed with the Grande Arche de La Défense. The 8km-long (5-mile) *Grand Axe* (Great Axis) runs from here to the Louvre's Pyramid.

9 General Marceau's Funeral

Marceau died in battle against the Austrian army in 1796, after a famous victory against them the previous year. His funeral is depicted in a frieze located above the *Departure of the Volunteers in 1792*.

10 Thirty Shields

Immediately below the top of the arch runs a row of 30 shields, each carrying the name of a Napoleonic victory.

NEED TO KNOW

MAP B2 ■ Pl Charles-de-Gaulle, 75008 ■ 01 55 37 73 77 (enquiries) ■ www.paris-arc-de-triomphe.fr/en

Open 10am–10:30pm (till 11pm Jun–Sep); booking a timed entry slot is essential

Adm €13 (under 18s, EU 18–25s free)

■ As part of ongoing plans to make the city greener for the 2024 Olympics, traffic lanes around the Arc de Triomphe will be reduced, creating more space for pedestrians around the arch.

■ Enjoy the old-world charm of Le Fouquet (99 Ave des Champs-Elysées).

■ Arch access is via the underground tunnel only.

TOP 10 ⭐ Centre Georges Pompidou

Today it's one of the world's most famous pieces of modern architecture. When the Pompidou Centre opened in 1977, however, architects Richard Rogers and Renzo Piano startled everyone by turning the building "inside out", with brightly coloured pipes displayed on the façade. Designed as a cross-cultural arts complex, it houses the excellent Musée National d'Art Moderne (Modern Art Museum), as well as two cinemas, a library, shops and performance space. The outside forecourt is a popular gathering spot for tourists and locals alike.

1 Pipes
Part of the shock factor of the Pompidou Centre is that the utility pipes are outside the building (below). Not only that, they are vividly coloured: bright green for water, yellow for electricity and blue for air conditioning.

5 Bookshop
The ground-floor bookshop sells a range of postcards, posters of major works in the Modern Art Museum and books on artists associated with Paris.

3 Escalator
One of the building's most striking and popular features is the external escalator (right) which climbs, snake-like, up the front of the Centre in its plexiglass tube. The view gets better and better as you rise high above the activity in the Centre's forecourt, before arriving at the top for the best view of all.

2 Top-Floor View
The view from the top of the Pompidou Centre is spectacular. The Eiffel Tower is visible, as is Montmartre in the north and the monolithic Tour Montparnasse to the south. On clear days views can stretch as far as La Défense (see p155).

4 The Piazza
Visitors and locals gather in the open space in front of the Centre to enjoy a variety of street performers and the changing installations of sculptures, which are often related to shows at the Centre.

6 Stravinsky Fountain
This colourful fountain in Place Igor Stravinsky was designed by Niki de Saint-Phalle and Jean Tinguely as part of the Pompidou Centre development. Inspired by composer Stravinsky's ballet The Firebird (1910), the bird spins and sprays water.

⑧ Avec l'arc noir (With a Black Arch)

One of the pioneers of Abstract art, artist Vasily Kandinsky (1866–1944) promoted the use of non-naturalist geometric forms. His *Avec l'arc noir* (1912) features a black line that recalls the *douga* (wooden arch) of a Russian *troika* (carriage).

⑦ Man with a Guitar

Within the Modern Art Museum, this 1914 work **(above)** by artist Georges Braque (1882–1963) is one of the most striking of the Cubist Movement.

NEED TO KNOW

MAP P2 ■ Pl Georges Pompidou 75004 ■ 01 44 78 12 33 ■ www. centrepompidou.fr

Museum: 11am–9pm Wed–Mon (to 11pm Thu); closed 1 May; adm €15–$17; free 1st Sun of the month, under-18s free, under-26s (EU only) free

Brancusi's Studio: 2–6pm Wed–Mon

■ The centre's café has free Wi-Fi access. For something grander, head to Georges, the rooftop brasserie.

■ Pre-booking a timed entry slot online is recommended.

Centre Guide

The Centre is home to various institutions. The Museum of Modern Art (Mnam) is on levels 4 and 5, and there is a cinema on level 1 and in the basement. Check at the information desk or on the website for details about the temporary shows (level 6), rehangs of works and the contemporary art "happenings". Displays at the Mnam often change and some works are now shared with its sister institution in Metz.

⑨ Brancusi's Studio

The Romanian sculptor Constantin Brancusi (1876–1957) left his entire studio to the state. It has been reconstructed **(left)** in the Piazza, and displays his abstract works.

⑩ Compositie n°3

Together with Piet Mondrian, Dutch painter Bart van der Leck (1876–1958) founded the De Stijl style, an abstract approach in which colours are limited and forms created with horizontal and vertical lines. The figurative basis for his work *Compositie n°3* is believed to have been harvesters.

TOP 10 ⭐ The Panthéon

Paris's Panthéon is a fitting final resting place for the nation's great figures. Originally built as a church at the behest of Louis XV, it was completed in 1790 and was intended to look like the Pantheon in Rome, but more closely resembles St Paul's Cathedral in London. During the Revolution it was used as a mausoleum. Napoleon returned it to the Church in 1806 and it became a public building in 1885.

1 Crypt
The crypt **(above)** is eerily impressive in its scale, compared to most tiny, dark church crypts. Here lie the tombs and memorials to worthy French citizens, including the prolific French writer Emile Zola (see p49).

2 Frescoes of Sainte Geneviève
Delicate murals by 19th-century artist Pierre Puvis de Chavannes, on the south wall of the nave, tell the story of Sainte Geneviève, the patron saint of Paris. She is believed to have saved the city from invasion in 451 by Attila the Hun and his hordes through the power of her prayers.

3 Façade
The Panthéon's façade **(right)** was inspired by Roman architecture. The 22 Corinthian columns support both the portico roof and bas-reliefs.

4 Dome
Inspired by Sir Christopher Wren's design for St Paul's Cathedral in London, as well as by the Dôme Church at Les Invalides (see p38), this iron-framed dome **(right)** is made up of three layers. At the top, a narrow opening lets in only a tiny amount of natural light, in keeping with the building's sombre purpose.

5 Dome Galleries
A staircase leads to the galleries immediately below the dome itself, affording spectacular 360-degree panoramic views of Paris. The pillars surrounding the galleries are both decorative and functional, providing essential support for the dome.

6 Women's Tombs
The first woman of colour (and one of only six women in all), actor and dancer Josephine Baker was interred here in 2021.

7 Foucault's Pendulum

In 1851 French physicist Jean Foucault (1819–68) followed up an earlier experiment to prove the Earth's rotation by hanging his famous pendulum from the dome of the Panthéon. The plane of the pendulum's swing rotated 11° clockwise each hour in relation to the floor, thereby proving Foucault's theory.

LOUIS BRAILLE

One of the most influential citizens buried in the Panthéon is Louis Braille (1809–52). Braille became blind at the age of three. He attended the National Institute for the Young Blind and was a gifted student. He continued at the Institute as a teacher and, in 1829, had the idea of adapting a coding system in use by the army, by turning words and letters into raised dots on card. Reading Braille has transformed the lives of blind people ever since.

The Panthéon

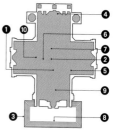

NEED TO KNOW

MAP N6 ■ Pl du Panthéon, 75005 ■ 01 44 32 18 00 ■ www.paris-pantheon.fr/en

Open Apr–Sep: 10am–6:30pm daily (Oct–Mar: to 6pm); closed 1 Jan, 1 May, 25 Dec

Adm €11.50 (under-18s & EU under-26s free)

■ Stop at La Crêperie *(12 Rue Soufflot; open 7am–midnight, from 8am Sun)* for crêpes or coffee.

■ Pre-booking a timed entry slot online is advisable.

■ From April to October, visitors can visit the dome for an extra fee.

8 Pediment Relief

The bas-relief above the entrance shows a female figure, representing France, handing out laurels to the great men of the nation – the same way that Greeks and Romans honoured their heroes.

9 Tomb of Voltaire

A statue **(left)** of the great writer, wit and philosopher Voltaire (1694–1788) stands in front of his tomb.

10 Tomb of Victor Hugo

The body of the French author *(see p23)* was carried to the Panthéon in a pauper's hearse, at his own request.

TOP 10 ⭐ Sainte-Chapelle

This Gothic masterpiece is considered the most beautiful church in Paris, not least for its renovated 15 stained-glass windows soaring 15 m (50 ft) to a star-covered vaulted ceiling. It was built by Louis IX (1214–70) as a shrine for his holy relics of the Passion and completed in 1248. The church was damaged during the 1789 Revolution but restored in the mid-19th century.

1 Window of Christ's Passion
Located above the apse, this stained-glass depiction of the Crucifixion is the most beautiful window in the chapel.

2 Lower Chapel
Intended for use by the king's servants, and dedicated to the Virgin Mary, this chapel **(below)** is not as light and lofty as the Upper Chapel but is still a magnificent sight.

5 Upper Chapel Entrance
As you emerge, via a spiral staircase, into this airy space **(right)**, the effect of light and colour is utterly breath-taking. The 13th-century stained-glass windows, the oldest surviving in Paris, separated by stone columns, depict biblical scenes from Genesis right through to the Crucifixion. To "read" the windows, start in the lower left panel and follow each row left to right, from bottom to top.

6 The Spire
The open latticework and pencil-thin shape give the *flèche* (spire) a very delicate appearance. In fact, three earlier church spires burned down – this one was erected in 1853 and rises 75 m (245 ft) into the air.

3 Main Portal
Like the Upper Chapel, the main portal has two tiers. Its pinnacles are decorated with a crown of thorns as a symbol of the relics within.

4 Rose Window
The Flamboyant rose window **(right)**, depicting St John's vision of the Apocalypse in 86 panels, was a gift from Charles VIII in 1485. The green and yellow hues are brightest at sunset.

7 St Louis' Oratory

In the late 14th century Louis XI added an oratory where he could watch Mass through a small grille in the wall. The chapel originally adjoined the Conciergerie, the former royal palace on the Ile de la Cité *(see p79)*.

9 Seats of the Royal Family

During Mass, the royal family sat in niches located in the fourth bays on both sides of the chapel, away from the congregation.

RELICS OF THE PASSION

Louis IX, later St Louis, was the only French king to be canonized. While on his first Crusade in 1239, he purchased the alleged Crown of Thorns from the Emperor of Constantinople, and subsequently other relics, including pieces of the True Cross, nails from the Crucifixion and a few drops of Christ's blood, paying almost three times more for them than for the construction of Sainte-Chapelle itself. The relics resided in Notre-Dame and were rescued from the destructive fire in 2019.

8 Evening Concerts

Sainte-Chapelle has excellent acoustics. From March until December, classical concerts are held here several evenings a week.

10 Apostle Statues

Beautifully carved medieval statues of 12 apostles stand on the pillars along the walls. Badly damaged in the Revolution, most have been restored: the bearded apostle **(right)**, fifth on the left, is the only original statue.

NEED TO KNOW

MAP N3 ◼ 6 Blvd du Palais, 75001 ◼ 01 53 40 60 97 ◼ www.sainte-chapelle.fr/en

Open Apr–Sep: 9am–7pm daily (Oct–Mar: to 5pm) (Opening hours can vary, check website for details)

Adm €11.50; under-18s and 18–25s

(EU only) free; audio guides €3; €18.50, joint adm to Conciergerie *(see p79)*; pre-booking a timed entry slot online is advisable.

◼ To experience a little 1920s-style elegance, try the old-fashioned Brasserie Les Deux Palais on the corner of the Boulevard du Palais and Rue de Lutèce for traditional Parisian fare.

◼ A pair of binoculars comes in handy if you want to catch a glimpse of the church's uppermost glass panels.

TOP 10 ⭐ Hôtel des Invalides

The *"invalides"* for whom this imposing Hôtel was built were wounded soldiers of the late 17th century. Louis XIV had the building constructed between 1671 and 1678, and veterans are still housed here, although only a dozen or so compared to the original 4,000. They share their home with arguably the most famous French soldier of them all, Napoleon Bonaparte, whose body rests in a crypt directly below the golden dome of the Dôme Church. Other buildings accommodate military offices, the Musée de l'Armée and smaller military museums.

1 Invalides Gardens

The approach to the Hôtel is across public gardens and then through a gate into the Invalides Gardens themselves. Designed in 1704, their paths are lined by 17th- and 18th-century cannons.

3 Golden Dome

The second church at the hôtel was begun in 1677 and took 27 years to build. Its magnificent dome stands 107 m (351 ft) high and glistens as much now as it did when Louis XIV, the Sun King, had it first gilded in 1715.

4 Musée de l'Armée

The Army Museum *(see p119)* is one of the largest collections of militaria in the world **(left)**. Enthusiasts will be absorbed for hours, and even the casual visitor will be fascinated by the exhibits. The Département Moderne, which traces military history from Louis XIV to Napoleon III, is also worth a visit.

Dôme Church Ceiling 2

The colourful, circular painting on the interior of the dome **(right)** above the crypt is the *Saint Louis in Glory* painted in 1692 by the French artist Charles de la Fosse. Near the centre is St Louis, who represents Louis XIV, presenting his sword to Christ in the presence of the Virgin Mary and angels.

7 Napoleon's Tomb

Napoleon's body was brought here from St Helena in 1840, some 19 years after he died. He rests in grandeur in a cocoon of six coffins **(left)**, almost "on the banks of the Seine", as was his last wish.

Hôtel des Invalides

5 Hôtel des Invalides

One of the loveliest sights in Paris, the Classical façade of the Hôtel **(below)** is four floors high and 196 m (645 ft) end to end. Features include the dormer windows with their variously shaped shield surrounds.

8 Church Tombs

Encircling the Dôme Church are the imposing tombs of great French military men, such as Marshal Foch and Marshal Vauban, who revolutionized military fortifications and siege tactics.

9 St-Louis-des-Invalides

Adjoining the Dôme Church is the Invalides complex's original church, worth seeing for its 17th-century organ, on which the first performance of Berlioz's *Requiem* was given.

10 Musée des Plans-Reliefs

Maps and models of French forts and fortified towns are displayed here. Some of them are beautifully detailed, such as the oldest model on display, of Perpignan, dating from 1686.

6 Musée de l'Ordre de la Libération

The Order of Liberation, France's highest military honour, was created by Général de Gaulle in 1940 to acknowledge contributions during World War II. The museum details the history of the honour and the wartime Free French movement.

NEED TO KNOW

MAP D4 ■ 129 Rue de Grenelle, 75007 or 6 Blvd des Invalides, 75007 ■ 01 44 42 38 77 ■ www.musee-armee.fr

Open 10am–6pm daily (to 9pm Tue during temporary exhibitions); closed 1 Jan, 1 May, 25 Dec; pre-booking a timed entry slot online is recommended

Adm €14; under-18s free; under-26s (EU only) free; audio guides €5

■ Le Café du Musée, between the Varenne metro station and the Musée Rodin *(see p120)*, is known for its varied menu of delicious cocktails, wines and beers. It is a lovely spot for a drink break.

Hôtel Guide

Approach from the Seine for the best view, and then walk around to the ticket office on the south side. You will need a ticket for the museums and to see Napoleon's Tomb. If time is short, concentrate on the Musée de l'Armée, before walking through to the cobbled courtyard in front of the Dôme Church.

The Top 10
of Everything

The elaborate interior of the Opéra National de Paris Garnier

Moments in History	42	Off the Beaten Track	58
Historic Buildings	44	Children's Attractions	60
Places of Worship	46	Entertainment Venues	64
Novels Set in Paris	48	Fine Dining	66
Museums	50	Cafés and Bars	68
Art Galleries	52	Shops and Markets	70
Riverfront Sights	54	Paris for Free	72
Parks and Gardens	56	Festivals and Events	74

🔟 Moments in History

1 Arrival of the Parisii

Although the remains of Neolithic settlements have been found dating back to 4500 BCE, the first inhabitants are considered to be a Celtic tribe called the Parisii, who settled on the Île de la Cité in the 3rd century BCE. Hunters and fishermen, they named their village Lutetia, meaning "boatyard on a river". The tribe minted their own gold coins and a pagan altar has been found beneath Notre-Dame.

2 Roman Settlement

The Romans conquered the Parisii in 52 BCE and rebuilt their city as an administrative centre on the Left Bank. The baths in the Musée National du Moyen Age *(see p50)* and the amphitheatre in Rue Monge are the only remains of the city's Roman incarnation as Lutetia. In 360 CE the Roman prefect was declared emperor and Lutetia was renamed Paris, after its original inhabitants.

3 Founding of France

Roman rule weakened under barbarian attacks. In 450 the prayers of a young nun, Geneviève, were credited with saving the city from invasion by Attila the Hun. She became the patron saint of Paris. But in 476 the Franks captured the city, Christianity became the official religion and Paris the capital of their new kingdom, France.

4 Charlemagne, Holy Roman Emperor

In 751 the Carolingian dynasty became rulers of France when Pepin the Short ascended the throne. His heir Charlemagne was crowned Holy Roman Emperor in 800 and moved the capital to Aix-la-Chapelle (now the city of Aachen). Paris fell into decline until Hugues Capet became king in 987, moving the capital back to his home city.

St Bartholomew's Day Massacre

5 St Bartholomew's Day Massacre

Catherine de Médicis, Henri II's queen, bore three French kings and one queen, Marguerite de Valois, who married the Protestant Henri of Navarre in August 1572. Catherine plotted to massacre the Protestant nobles who attended the wedding. The killings began on 24 August and thousands died. Henri of Navarre survived and later became Henri IV, the first Bourbon king.

6 French Revolution

Following decades of royal excess and the growing gulf between rich and poor, Paris erupted into Revolution with the storming of the Bastille prison in 1789.

Ste Geneviève, patron saint of Paris

7 Napoleon's Coronation

As Paris rose from the ashes of Revolution, a young general from Corsica, Napoleon Bonaparte *(see p22)*, saved the city from a royalist revolt, then led military victories in Italy and Egypt. He crowned himself Emperor of France in Notre-Dame in 1804.

8 The Second Empire

In 1851, Napoleon's nephew, Louis-Napoleon, seized power as Emperor Napoleon III. He appointed Baron Haussmann to oversee the massive building and public works projects that transformed Paris into the most glorious city in Europe. The wide boulevards, many public buildings, parks, the sewer system and the first department stores date from between 1852 and 1870.

9 The Paris Commune

Following France's defeat in the Franco-Prussian War *(see p27)* in 1871, many citizens rejected the harsh terms of the surrender and a left-wing group revolted, setting up the Paris Commune. But, after 72 days, government troops marched on the city. In a week of brutal street fighting (21–28 May), much of the city burned and thousands of rebellious citizens were killed.

10 Liberation of Paris

The occupation of France by Germany during World War II was a dark period for Paris. The city was the centre for the French Resistance. Allied forces liberated Paris on 25 August 1944; just two days earlier, the German commander Von Choltitz had ignored Adolf Hitler's order to burn the city to the ground.

The Liberation of Paris

TOP 10 EVENTS IN THE FRENCH REVOLUTION

Storming of the Bastille

1 14 July 1789
The storming of the Bastille prison, a symbol of repression, launches the Revolution.

2 4 August 1789
The abolition of feudalism, and the right of everyone to be a free citizen, is declared.

3 26 August 1789
Formal declaration of the Rights of Man and the Citizen, which incorporated the ideals of equality and dignity, later subsumed into the 1791 Constitution.

4 October 1789
Citizens march on Versailles and the royal family returns to Paris to be imprisoned in the Tuileries Palace.

5 20 June 1791
King Louis XVI and his family try to escape but are spotted in Varenne and return to Paris as captives.

6 10 August 1792
A mob storms the Tuileries and the royals are imprisoned in the Temple.

7 21 September 1792
The monarchy is formally abolished and the First Republic is proclaimed.

8 1792–4
"The Terror" reigns, under the radical Commune led by Robespierre, Danton and Marat. Thousands are executed by guillotine.

9 21 January 1793
Louis XVI is found guilty of treason and executed. His queen Marie-Antoinette follows him to the guillotine on 16 October.

10 28 July 1794
Robespierre is guillotined, marking the end of The Terror, and the Revolution draws to a close.

Top 10 Historic Buildings

1 Hôtel des Invalides

See pp38–9.

2 Versailles

Louis XIV turned his father's old hunting lodge into the largest palace *(see p155)* in Europe and moved his court here in 1678. It was the royal residence for more than a century until Louis XVI and his queen Marie-Antoinette fled during the Revolution.

3 Conciergerie

Originally home to the keeper of the king's mansion and guards of the Palais de Justice, the Conciergerie *(see p79)* became a prison at the end of the 14th century. More than 4,000 citizens (including Marie-Antoinette) were held prisoner here during the Revolution, half of whom were guillotined. It remained a prison until 1914.

4 Hôtel de Ville

MAP P3 ■ 4 Pl de l'Hôtel de Ville, 75001 ■ 01 42 76 40 40 ■ Open for group tours and temporary exhibitions (booking essential: 01 42 76 54 04)

Paris's city hall sports an elaborate façade, with ornate stonework, statues and a turreted roof. It is a 19th-century reconstruction of the original town hall, which was burned down during the Paris Commune *(see p43)* of 1871. Though the square in front is pleasant now, it was once the site of executions: Ravaillac, assassin of Henri IV, was quartered alive here in 1610.

Interior of the Hôtel de la Marine

5 Hôtel de la Marine

MAP D3 ■ 2 Place de la Concorde, 75008 ■ www.hotel-de-la-marine.paris ■ Open 10:30am-7pm daily (Fri till 9.30pm)

The Hôtel de la Marine is a splendid colonnaded 18th-century building, which used to be the royal Garde Meuble (storehouse) and then the ministry of naval affairs. Its beautiful reception rooms and apartments have been restored and are now open to the public.

6 Palais de Justice

The enormous building that now houses the French law courts *(see p80)* and judiciary dates back to the Roman times and was the royal

Hôtel de Ville façade

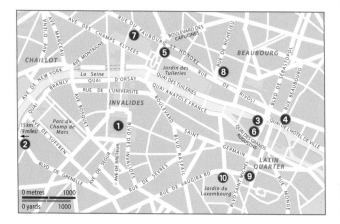

palace until the 14th century, when Charles V moved the court to the Marais. During the Revolution, thousands were sentenced to death in the Première Chambre Civile, allegedly the former bedroom of Louis IX.

7 Palais de l'Elysée

This imposing palace *(see p113)* has been the official residence of the President of the French Republic since 1873. It was built as a private mansion in 1718 and was owned by Madame de Pompadour, mistress of Louis XV, who extended the English-style gardens as far as the Champs-Elysées. After the Battle of Waterloo in 1815, Napoleon signed his second and final abdication here.

8 Palais-Royal

This former royal palace *(see p104)*, originally called the Palais-Cardinal, now houses State offices. It was built by Cardinal Richelieu in 1632, passing to the Crown on his death 10 years later, and was the childhood home of Louis XIV. The dukes of Orléans acquired it in the 18th century.

9 La Sorbonne

The city's great university *(see p125)* had humble beginnings in 1253 as a college for 16 poor students to study theology. France's first printing house was also established here in 1469. After suppression during the Revolution it became the University of Paris.

10 Palais du Luxembourg

MAP L6 ■ 15 Rue de Vaugirard, 75006 ■ 01 42 34 20 00 ■ Open for reserved group tours only (visites@senat.fr); gardens: open dawn–dusk daily

Marie de Médicis had architect Salomon de Brosse model this palace after her childhood home, the Pitti Palace in Florence. Shortly after its completion she was exiled by her son, Louis XIII. It was seized from the Crown during the Revolution to become a prison and it now houses the French Senate. Nearby is the Musée du Luxembourg.

Palais du Luxembourg

🔟 Places of Worship

1 Notre-Dame
See pp20–23.

2 Sacré-Coeur
See pp26–7.

3 Sainte-Chapelle
Although this lovely chapel *(see pp36–7)* is no longer used for worship, the soaring stained-glass windows encourage reverence.

4 Eglise du Dôme
The final resting place of Napoleon Bonaparte is the beautiful Dôme Church in the Hôtel des Invalides *(see pp38–9)* complex – an elaborate monument in French Classical style. Built as the chapel for the resident soldiers of the Invalides, its ornate high altar is in stark contrast to the solemn marble chapels surrounding the crypt, which hold the tombs of French military leaders. Its golden dome can be seen for miles around.

5 St-Eustache
For centuries, this Gothic edifice *(see p85)* was the market church serving the traders of Les Halles. Taking more than 100 years to build, it was finally completed in 1637 and its cavernous interior displays the architectural style of the early Renaissance. Popular Sunday afternoon organ recitals and other classical concerts take place in this wonderfully atmospheric setting.

Façade of La Madeleine

6 La Madeleine
MAP D3 ■ Pl de la Madeleine, 75008 ■ Open 9:30am–7pm daily (services vary)
Designed in the style of a Greek temple in 1764, this prominent church in Paris's financial district, on the edge of the Opéra Quarter, is one of the city's most distinctive sights, spectacularly surrounded by 52 Corinthian columns. The church was consecrated to Mary Magdalene in 1845. The bronze doors, which include bas-reliefs of the Ten Commandments, and the Last Judgment on the south pediment, are exterior highlights, while the ornate marble and gold interior has many fine statues, including François Rude's *Baptism of Christ*. It is also a popular venue for classical concerts.

7 The Panthéon
Modelled on the Pantheon in Rome, this domed late 18th-century church *(see pp34–5)* only served as a house of worship for two years, before becoming a monument and burial place for the great and the good of

St-Eustache

the Revolution era. Later distinguished citizens are also buried here.

⑧ Grande Synagogue de la Victoire

MAP E2 ▪ 44 Rue de la Victoire, 75009
▪ Open Mon–Fri mornings for group tours (call 01 45 26 95 36)

Built in the late 19th century, this elaborate synagogue is the second largest in Europe. The building is open only to those wishing to attend services and to groups who have arranged a visit in advance. Other smaller synagogues can be found in the Marais, which has long had a large Jewish community, including one at 10 rue Pavée, built in 1913 by Hector Guimard, the architect who designed the city's magnificent Art Nouveau metro stations.

⑨ Grande Mosquée de Paris

The city's Grand Mosque (see p136) was built during the 1920s as a tribute to North African Muslims who gave military support to France during World War I. Its beautiful Hispano-Moorish architecture, including a minaret, was executed by craftsmen brought over from North Africa. There is also a shaded interior courtyard where visitors can sit and sip a glass of mint tea.

⑩ St-Sulpice

Outstanding frescoes in the Chapel of the Angels by Eugène Delacroix are the highlight of this 17th-century church (see p125). With more than 6,500 pipes, its organ, designed by Jean-François Chalgrin in 1776, is one of the largest in the world. The novelist Victor Hugo married his childhood sweetheart Adèle Foucher here in 1822.

St-Sulpice church organ

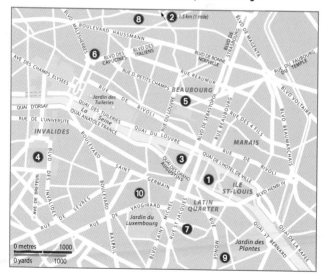

TOP 10 Novels Set in Paris

Performance of *Les Misérables*

1 Les Misérables

The 1862 novel by Victor Hugo (1802–85) is an all too vivid portrayal of the poor and the dispossessed in early 19th-century Paris. At its centre is the tale of nobleman Jean Valjean, unfairly victimized by an unjust system. The character of Marius, the young idealist, is based on Hugo's own experiences as an impoverished student.

2 The Hunchback of Notre-Dame

Better known by its English title, which inspired a film of the same name, Victor Hugo's Gothic novel was published in France in 1831 as *Notre-Dame de Paris (see p23)*. Set in the Middle Ages, it tells the strange and moving story of a hunchback bell-ringer, Quasimodo, and his love for Esmeralda.

3 A Tale of Two Cities

The finest chronicler of 19th-century London life, Charles Dickens (1812–70) chose to set his 1859 novel in London and Paris, against the background of the French Revolution *(see p43)*. His description of conditions in the Bastille prison makes for grim reading.

4 Le Père Goriot

Honoré de Balzac (1799–1850) chronicled Parisian life masterfully in his 80-volume *La comédie humaine* series, and this novel of 1835 is certainly among his finest. Balzac's former home *(see p142)* at 47 rue Raynouard in the 16th *arrondissement*, where he lived from 1840 to 1847, is open to the public.

5 Sentimental Education

Gustave Flaubert (1821–80) studied law in Paris but illness disrupted his chosen career and he devoted himself to literature. This work (*L'education sentimentale* in French), first published in 1870 in two volumes, stands alongside his greatest novel, *Madame Bovary* (1857), and marks the move away from Romanticism to Realism in French literature.

6 Bel-Ami

Guy de Maupassant (1850–93) published this, one of his best novels, in 1885, criticizing the get-rich-quick Parisian business world of the *belle époque*. Widely acknowledged as one of the world's greatest short-story writers, Maupassant is buried in the cemetery at Montparnasse *(see p156)* in Greater Paris.

Guy de Maupassant

7 A la Recherche du Temps Perdu

The master work of Marcel Proust (1871–1922) was written in 13 volumes, the first novel appearing in 1913. Proust lived on boulevard Haussmann, and his epic tale is the fictionalized story of his own life, and of Paris during the *belle époque*. Proust is buried in Père Lachaise Cemetery *(see p156)* in eastern Paris.

8 Suite Française

The German-occupied Paris of World War II is grippingly recounted in this 2004 bestseller by Ukranian-Jewish author Irène Nemirovsky (1903–42). She wrote her manuscript as the war raged; she was killed at Auschwitz. Her notebooks were redis-covered in the late 1990s, and the book was published to much acclaim.

9 A Certain Smile

Françoise Sagan (1935–2004) is perhaps best known for her scandalous 1954 novel, *Bonjour Tristesse*. Her 1955 novel *Un Certain Sourire*, which tells of a provincial Sorbonne student who has an affair with a married man, followed in a similar, deliciously wicked vein, its narrator another bold young woman who refused to subscribe to the morals and expectations of a patriarchal society.

10 Nana

Perhaps the greatest Parisian chronicler of them all, Emile Zola (1840–1902) was born, lived and died in the city, although he spent part of his youth in Aix-en-Provence in southern France. *Nana* was pub-lished in 1880 and tells a shocking tale of sexual decadence through the eyes of the central character, an actress and sex worker.

Painting of *Nana* by Edouard Manet

TOP 10 FOREIGN WRITERS WHO LIVED IN PARIS

Ernest Hemingway

1 Ernest Hemingway
The US author (1899–1961) wrote *A Moveable Feast* as an affectionate portrait of his time living in Paris from 1921 to 1926.

2 F. Scott Fitzgerald
Like Hemingway, US writer Fitzgerald (1896–1940) lived in Montparnasse and frequented La Coupole *(see p131)*.

3 George Orwell
The English novelist (1903–50) tells of his shocking experiences living in poverty in *Down and Out in Paris and London* (1933).

4 Samuel Beckett
The Irish-born playwright (1906–89) lived in Paris from 1928 until his death.

5 Anaïs Nin
US novelist Nin (1903–77) met her lover, fellow American Henry Miller, in Paris. Her *Diaries* tell of her time here.

6 Albert Camus
Algerian-born Camus (1913–60) moved to Paris in 1935 and lived here until his death.

7 Henry Miller
Miller (1891–1980) showed the seedier side of Paris in his novel *Tropic of Cancer* (1934).

8 Nancy Mitford
The author of *The Pursuit of Love* (1945) and other novels, Mitford (1904–73) lived in Paris from 1943 until her death.

9 James Joyce
Joyce (1882–1941) lived in Paris from 1920 to 1940. *Ulysses* was published here in 1922 by Shakespeare and Co.

10 Milan Kundera
Czech-born Kundera (b.1929) moved to Paris in 1978, writing *The Unbearable Lightness of Being* here.

🔟 Museums

The Lady and the Unicorn,
Musée National du Moyen Age

1 Musée National du Moyen Age

This remarkable museum *(see p126)* dedicated to the art of the Middle Ages is known by several names. This includes the Musée de Cluny, after the beautiful mansion in which it is housed, and the Thermes de Cluny, after the Roman baths adjoining the museum. Highlights include the famous "Lady and the Unicorn" tapestries, medieval stained glass and exquisite gold crowns and jewellery.

2 Musée de l'Armée

Part of the Hôtel des Invalides complex relating to the military history of France, this museum *(see pp38–9)* has a huge number of military objects from the Middle Ages to World War II. The collection includes armour, artillery, weapons, uniforms and paintings. Admission includes entrance to the Dôme Church, containing the tomb of Napoleon Bonaparte.

3 Musée des Arts Décoratifs

Set over nine levels, adjoining the west end of the Louvre's Richelieu Wing, this arts museum *(see p104)* showcases furniture and tableware from the 12th century to the present. The breathtaking anthology of pieces ranges from Gothic panelling and Renaissance porcelain to 1970s carpets and chairs by Philippe Starck. Also part of the museum is the Musée de la Mode et du Textile, which mounts fashion exhibitions, and the Musée de la Publicité, which has exhibitions on advertising.

4 Musée du Louvre

French and Italian sculpture, Greek and Roman antiquities and paintings from the 12th to the 19th centuries are just some of the highlights of the world's largest museum *(see pp12–15)*.

5 Musée du Quai Branly – Jacques Chirac

In a city dominated by Western art, this fabulous museum *(see p120)* tips the balance in favour of arts from Africa, Asia, Oceania and the Americas. Must-sees include the African instruments. The striking Jean Nouvel-designed building is an attraction in itself.

6 Muséum National d'Histoire Naturelle

Paris's Natural History Museum *(see p135)* in the Jardin des Plantes contains a fascinating collection of animal skeletons, plant fossils, minerals and gemstones. Its highlight is the magnificent Grande Galerie de l'Evolution *(see p60)*, which depicts the changing interaction between man and nature during the evolution of life on Earth.

Muséum National d'Histoire Naturelle

Musée des Arts et Métiers

7 Musée des Arts et Métiers

MAP G3 ■ 60 Rue Réaumur, 75003 ■ Open 10am–6pm Tue–Sun (to 9pm Fri) ■ Closed 1 Jan, 1 May, 25 Dec ■ Adm ■ www.arts-et-metiers.net

Housed in the Abbaye de St-Martins-des-Champs, this industrial design museum is a fascinating repository of printing machines, vintage cars, music boxes, early flying machines, automatons and other inventions.

8 Musée Carnavalet

The vast collection at this museum (see p94), refurbished in 2021, charts the history of Paris. The museum occupies two adjoining mansions – Carnavalet and Le Peletier de St-Fargeau – both decorated with gilded wood panelling, furniture and objets d'art, including paintings and sculptures of famous personalities, and engravings showing the creation of Paris.

9 Cité de l'Architecture et du Patrimoine

The Cité de l'Architecture (see p141) and the Musée des Monuments Français showcase French architectural heritage and form one of the world's foremost architectural centres. The Galerie des Moulages houses models of French cathedrals.

10 Musée Jacquemart-André

Set in a private mansion, this museum (see p113) was once the home of Edouard André and his artist wife Nélie Jacquemart. It houses their personal art collection, which features works by Boucher, Botticelli, Rembrandt and Fragonard, as well as excellent temporary exhibits.

Musée Jacquemart-André

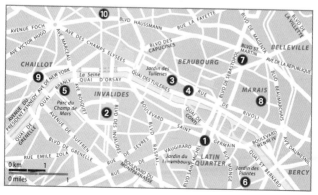

🔟 Art Galleries

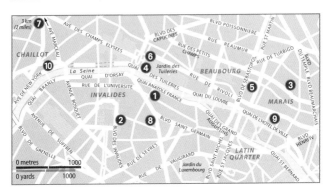

1️⃣ Musée d'Orsay
See pp16–19.

2️⃣ Musée Rodin
On a sunny day, head straight for the gardens of the Musée Rodin (see p120), next to the Hôtel des Invalides complex, to enjoy some of the French sculptor's most famous works, including *The Thinker* and *The Burghers of Calais*, while strolling among the shady trees and rose bushes. Auguste Rodin (1840–1917) lived and worked for nine years in the beautiful 18th-century Hôtel Biron, where the rest of the collection is housed. The elegant interiors

The Thinker, Musée Rodin

contain some of Rodin's best-known works such as *The Kiss*, as well as artworks that he collected.

3️⃣ Musée Picasso
The beautiful Hôtel Salé (see p96) showcases an extensive collection of paintings, sculptures, ceramics, etchings, drawings and other masterpieces by the famous Spanish-born artist Pablo Picasso (1881–1973) – covering all his creative periods. Large sculptures adorn the garden and courtyard while, inside the gorgeous 17th-century mansion (see p93), twice as much as before of the collection is now on display. Be sure not to miss Picasso's own collection of paintings, including works by Cézanne, Renoir, Matisse and others of his contemporaries, located on the second floor.

4️⃣ Musée de l'Orangerie
MAP D3 ▪ Jardin des Tuileries, 75001 ▪ Open 9am–6pm Wed–Mon ▪ Closed 1 May, 14 Jul (am), 25 Dec ▪ Adm ▪ www.musee-orangerie.fr

The prime exhibits here are eight of Monet's waterlily canvases (see p16), most of them painted between 1899 and 1921, and the gallery, located in a corner of the Tuileries. The Walter-Guillaume collection covers works by Matisse, Picasso, Modigliani and other modern masters from 1870 to 1930.

Pompidou Centre

5 Musée National d'Art Moderne

The revolutionary Pompidou Centre (see pp32–3) is the perfect home for France's incredible Modern Art Museum. It features around 15,000 fascinating works across several levels, with an exciting schedule of temporary exhibitions, gallery spaces and lecture programmes. Level 5 traces the history of modern art (between 1905 and 1965) before leading to the contemporary collection on level 4.

6 Jeu de Paume

MAP D3 ▪ 1 Pl de la Concorde, 75008 ▪ Opening hours are subject to change, check website ▪ Closed 1 Jan, 1 May, 25 Dec ▪ Adm ▪ www.jeudepaume.org

This gallery is a fine exhibition space, set within a former 19th-century royal tennis court (jeu de paume). It has a strong reputation for show-casing outstanding photography, film and video installations.

7 Fondation Louis Vuitton

8 Ave du Mahatma Gandhi, Bois de Boulogne, 75116 ▪ Opening hours vary according to exhibitions and events ▪ Adm ▪ www.fondationlouisvuitton.fr

Close to the Jardin d'Acclimatation in the Bois de Boulogne (see p159), Frank Gehry's dramatic glass structure contains a gallery and event space hosting arts exhibitions.

8 Musée Maillol

Works of the famous French artist Aristide Maillol, including his paintings and sculptures, are the focal point of this museum (see p127), which was created by his model, Dina Vierny (1919–2009). Other artists feature in the temporary exhibitions.

9 Maison Européenne de la Photographie

If you're a photography fan, be sure not to miss this splendid gallery (see p95) located in the Marais. Its exhibitions range from portraits to documentary work, retrospectives to contemporary photographers.

10 Palais de Tokyo

MAP B4 ▪ 13 Ave du Président Wilson, 75116 ▪ Open noon–midnight Wed–Mon ▪ Adm ▪ www.palaisdetokyo.com

Dedicated to contemporary art, this lively museum in the Chaillot Quarter hosts regularly changing exhibitions and installations by international artists. It is one of the most cutting-edge art houses in Europe and has a bookshop, two restaurants and a nightclub (YoYo).

ON AIR exhibition curated by Rebecca Lamarche-Vadel at Palais de Tokyo

🔟 Riverfront Sights

Eiffel Tower and the Seine, viewed from Pont Alexandre III

① Eiffel Tower

Although the top of the Eiffel Tower (see pp24–5) can be seen above rooftops across the city, one of the best views of this Paris landmark is from the Seine. The Pont d'Iéna lies at the foot of the tower, bridging the river to link it to the Trocadéro Gardens. The tower, illuminated at night, is a highlight of a dinner cruise on the Seine.

② Palais de Chaillot

The curved arms of the Palais de Chaillot (see p141) encircling the Trocadéro Gardens can be seen from the Seine. In the centre of the gardens magnificent fountains spout from the top of a long pool lined with statues, while two huge water cannons spray their charges back towards the river and the Eiffel Tower on the opposite bank.

③ Liberty Flame
MAP C3

A replica of the New York Statue of Liberty's torch was erected here in 1987 by the *International Herald Tribune* to mark their centenary and honour the freedom

fighters of the French Resistance during World War II. It is located on the right bank of the Pont de l'Alma, the bridge over the tunnel where Diana, Princess of Wales, was fatally injured in an automobile crash in 1997. The Liberty Flame has now become her unofficial memorial and is often draped with notes and flowers laid in her honour.

④ Grand Palais and Petit Palais

Gracing either side of the magnificent Pont Alexandre III are these two splendid exhibition halls (see p111), built for the Universal Exhibition of 1900. The iron Art Nouveau skeleton of the Grand Palais is topped by an enormous glass roof, which is most impressive when illuminated at night. The Petit Palais is smaller but similar in style, with a dome and many Classical features.

Liberty Flame by Pont de l'Alma

⑤ Pont Alexandre III

The most beautiful bridge (see p112) in Paris is the Pont Alexandre III, a riot of Art Nouveau decoration including

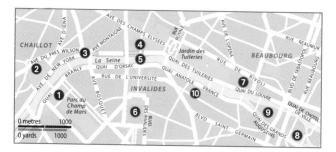

cherubs, wreaths, lamps and other elaborate statuary. Built for the Universal Exhibition of 1900, it leads to the Grand Palais and Petit Palais. There are wonderful views of the Invalides complex and the Champs-Elysées from the bridge.

6 Dôme Church

An impressive view of the Eglise de Dôme in the Hôtel des Invalides (see pp38–9) complex can be had from the Pont Alexandre III. The golden dome beckons visitors down the long parkway lined with streetlamps and statues.

7 Musée du Louvre

This grand museum (see pp12–15) stretches along the river from the Pont Royal to the Pont des Arts. The Denon Wing, which can be seen from the Seine, was largely built during the reigns of Henri IV and Louis XIII in the late 16th and early 17th centuries.

8 Notre-Dame

The great cathedral, although damaged (see pp20–23), is still majestic when viewed from the Left Bank of the Seine. It rises at the eastern end of the Ile de la Cité above the remains of the ancient tribes who first settled Paris in the 3rd century BCE.

9 Conciergerie

This huge and imposing building (see p79), which served as a notorious prison during the French Revolution, commands the western end of the Ile de la Cité. The magnificent building retains some of the few medieval features on the island, including a torture chamber, kitchens, a clock and the twin towers that rise above the Quai de l'Horloge.

10 Musée d'Orsay

The view of this stunning art gallery (see pp16–19) from the Right Bank of the Seine is one of its finest angles, showing off the arched terminals, great clock faces and grand façade of this former railway station, built in 1898–1900. Architect Victor Laloux designed it to harmonize with the Louvre and Tuileries Quarter across the river.

Sculptures at Musée d'Orsay

TOP 10 Parks and Gardens

Stately Palais du Luxembourg in the Jardin du Luxembourg

1 Jardin du Luxembourg

Parisians love this centrally located park *(see p125)*, set around the Palais du Luxembourg. The sweeping terrace is a great place for people-watching, while locals sunbathe around the octagonal Grand Bassin or sail toy boats in the water. Statues are dotted throughout the grounds, and there is a café.

2 Jardin des Tuileries

Now officially part of the Louvre, these gardens *(see p103)* were laid out in the 17th century as part of the old Palais de Tuileries. They stretch along the Seine between the Louvre and Place de la Concorde. The walkways are lined with lime and chestnut trees. Statues include bronze figures by Aristide Maillol.

3 Jardin des Plantes

Established as a medicinal herb garden for the king in 1635, these vast botanical gardens *(see p135)* are a wonderfully tranquil spot. Paths are lined with statuary and mature trees and there are some glasshouses, including one devoted to the flora of Nouvelle Caledonie.

4 Bois de Boulogne

At the weekends, Parisians head for this vast park *(see p156)* on the western edge of the city, which has a boating lake and paths for cycling, jogging and strolling. There are three formal gardens, lakes and waterfalls, and even two horse-racing tracks. It's a good spot for a break from the city bustle.

5 Bois de Vincennes

Another great escape from the city, this vast park *(see p156)* is to the east of Paris what the Bois de Boulogne is to the west. A former royal hunting ground, it was landscaped in the 1860s. Now it features ornamental lakes, the beautiful Parc Floral *(see p59)*, a zoo and a spring funfair.

6 Parc Monceau

The most fashionable green space *(see p157)* in Paris, full of well-heeled residents of the nearby mansions and apartments. The lush landscaping dates from

Classical colonnade in Parc Monceau

the 18th century, and some architectural follies, such as the Classical colonnade, survive.

7 Jardin du Palais-Royal
MAP L1 ■ Pl du Palais-Royal, 75001

These lovely gardens are enclosed by the 18th-century arcades of the Palais-Royal (see p104). Modern sculptures include Daniel Buren's controversial striped columns.

8 Parc Clichy-Batignolles
147 Rue Cardinet, 75017 ■ Metro Brochant

A relaxed, neighbourhood feel characterizes this park in the heart of the laid-back Batignolles district. It was developed with an eye to ecology and biodiversity. Locals come to skate, play *pétanque*, tend the community gardens and laze on the lawns, while wildlife and rare flora thrive in the wetlands-like environment.

9 Parc Montsouris
Blvd Jourdan, 75014 ■ RER Cité Universitaire

Located south of Montparnasse, this large park in central Paris was laid out in the English style, atop an old granite quarry, by landscape architect Adolphe Alphand between 1865 and 1878. Hemingway (see p49) and other writers and artists frequented the park in the mid-20th century. It has a jogging path, lake and a bandstand.

10 Parc des Buttes-Chaumont
Rue Manin, 75019 ■ Metro Buttes-Chaumont ■ Open Sep–Apr: 7am–8pm daily; May–Aug: 7am–10pm Mon–Fri, 24 hours Sat & Sun

Baron Haussmann created this retreat (see p61) northeast of the city centre in 1867, from what was formerly a rubbish dump. His architects built artificial cliffs, waterfalls, streams and a lake complete with an island crowned by a Roman-style temple. There are fantastic views of the city from this hilly park. In the eastern part of the park is a trendy bar, Rosa Bonheur, which is open until late.

TOP 10 FOUNTAINS

Observatory Fountain

1 Observatory Fountain
MAP L6 ■ Jardin du Luxembourg
Four bronze statues representing the continents hold aloft a globe.

2 Four Seasons Fountain
MAP C4 ■ Rue de Grenelle
Paris in female form looks down on figures representing the Seine and Marne rivers, designed in 1739 by sculptor Edmé Bouchardon.

3 Fontaine des Innocents
Carved by Jean Goujon in 1547, this (see p86) is Paris's only Renaissance fountain.

4 Medici Fountain
MAP L6 ■ Jardin du Luxembourg
This ornate 17th-century fountain with a pond was built for Marie de Médicis.

5 Molière Fountain
MAP E3 ■ Rue de Richelieu
This 19th-century fountain honours the French playwright.

6 Agam Fountain
La Défense ■ RER La Défense
Architect Yaacov Agam designed this fountain of water and lights.

7 Châtelet Fountain
MAP N3 ■ Pl du Châtelet
The two sphinxes of this 1808 fountain are appropriate to commemorate Napoleon's campaign in Egypt.

8 Stravinsky Fountain
Birds squirt water from this colourful Pompidou Centre fountain (see p32).

9 Trocadéro Fountains
Spouting towards the Eiffel Tower (see pp24–5), these fountains are illuminated at night.

10 Versailles Fountains
The fountains at Versailles (see p155) flow to music at weekends in spring and in summer.

🔟 Off the Beaten Track

Wall of skulls and bones, Catacombs

1 Catacombs
1 Ave du Colonel Henri Rol-Tanguy, 75014 ▪ 01 43 22 47 63 ▪ Open 9:45am–8:30pm Tue–Sun ▪ Closed 1 Jan, 1 May, 25 Dec ▪ Adm ▪ www.catacombes.paris.fr

The catacombs are an underground warren of tunnels, filled with the bones of some six million Parisians, brought here from 1785 to 1865 as a solution to the problem of overflowing cemeteries. Aside from the macabre sight of walls lined with skulls and bones, it's a thrill to enter the tunnels, part of a vast quarry network that underlies the city. Limited numbers of visitors are allowed in at a time; pre-book a timed entry slot online.

2 Promenade Plantée
MAP H5

Starting near the Bastille Opera House (see p65) and ending at Bois de Vincennes, this 4-km (2.5-mile) walkway, some of it high above the streets on a former railway viaduct, is a wonderful way to see a little-visited part of the city. Planted all along with trees and flowers, the path runs past tall mansion blocks, whose decorative mouldings and balconies (not to mention smart interiors) are a treat to see close up.

3 Little-visited Louvre
While many flock to the *Mona Lisa* and *Venus de Milo*, canny visitors set out to discover other parts of the Louvre's collections (see pp12–15), such as the Islamic arts section. It includes beautiful Iznik tiles and exquisite glass, gold and ivory objects from Andalusia, Iraq and India – all under a stunning gold filigree roof.

4 Pavillon de l'Arsenal
MAP R5 ▪ 21 Blvd Morland, 75004 ▪ 01 42 76 33 97 ▪ Open 11am–7pm Tue–Sun ▪ www.pavillon-arsenal.com

A museum dedicated to urban planning and architecture, the Pavillon de l'Arsenal is home to a small but fascinating exhibition illustrating the architectural evolution of Paris. Using film, models and panoramic photographs, it explores how the city has developed over the centuries and what future plans hold.

5 Canal Barge Cruise
MAP J2 ▪ 12 Port de Solferino, 75007 ▪ Cruises dates vary, check website ▪ Adm ▪ www.pariscanal.com

A great way to see a different side of Paris is to take a barge along the Seine, the Marne river and Canal St-Martin. Some Paris Canal boats, for example, depart from the quay

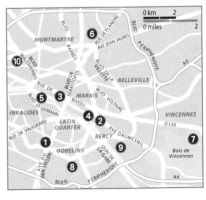

outside the Musée d'Orsay (see pp16–19) and make their way westwards to the island of Chatou, once frequented by Impressionist painters, or eastwards past Notre-Dame to Chennevières-sur-Marne, a favourite haunt of Pissaro.

Barge on Canal St-Martin

⑥ Le Centquatre-Paris
5 Rue Curial, 75019 ■ 01 53 35 50 00 ■ Metro Riquet ■ Open noon–7pm Tue–Fri, 11am–7pm Sat & Sun ■ www.104.fr

The "104" is a huge arts centre, housed in a converted 19th-century funeral parlour with a lofty glass roof. It contains numerous artists' studios and workshops, and puts on excellent exhibitions and installations, as well as music, dance, cinema and theatre.

⑦ Parc Floral de Paris
Route de la Pyramide, 75012 ■ Metro Chateau de Vincennes ■ Open 9:30am–8pm daily (winter: to dusk) ■ Adm Jun–Sep ■ www.parcfloraldeparis.com

Set within the Bois de Vincennes, this lovely park has wonderful displays of camellias, rhododendrons, ferns and irises. It hosts horticultural exhibitions and free jazz concerts in summer and has plenty to appeal to children, including an adventure park.

⑧ Buttes-aux-Cailles
Metro Corvisart

The Butte-aux-Cailles quarter, in the southeast of the city, is a bit like a mini-Montmartre, with its pretty cobbled streets and old-fashioned streetlamps. The main Rue de la Butte-aux-Cailles with its restaurants and bohemian bars buzzes well into the night.

⑨ Bercy Village
28 Rue François Truffaut, 75012 ■ Metro Cour St-Emilion ■ www.bercyvillage.com

The district of Bercy is where barges from all over France used to deliver wine to the capital. The former warehouses, a handsome ensemble of ochre-coloured stone buildings, have been converted into shops, restaurants and, fittingly, wine bars. It's well worth a wander, especially on Sundays when shops in most other parts of Paris are closed.

⑩ Musée Nissim de Camondo
MAP C2 ■ 63 Rue de Monceau, 75008 ■ 01 44 55 57 50 ■ Open 10am–5:30pm Wed–Sun ■ Adm

Wealthy art collector Count Moïse de Camondo had this grand mansion built to house his superb collection of 18th-century art. The rooms are full of tapestries, paintings, gilded furniture and Sèvres porcelain. As interesting as the artworks is the portrait that emerges of a well-to-do family, beset by tragedy (it is named for his son, killed in World War I) and ultimately victim to Auschwitz.

Musée Nissim de Camondo

🔟 Children's Attractions

Musée de la Magie et des Automates

1 Musée de la Magie et des Automates

MAP R4 ▪ 11 Rue St-Paul, 75004 ▪ 01 42 72 13 26 ▪ Open 2–7pm Wed, Sat, Sun (daily during school holidays, except Jul & Aug) ▪ Adm ▪ www.museedelamagie.com

Kids are enchanted by this museum of magic, located in the cellars of the former home of the Marquis de Sade. Magicians conjure up shows every half hour involving optical illusions, card tricks and lots of audience participation. Exhibits include working automata and memorabilia of magicians such as Houdini (1874–1926).

2 Parc Astérix

Plailly, 60128 ▪ RER B to Roissy CDG1, then shuttle from A3 ▪ Open Apr–Aug: 10am–6pm Mon–Thu (to 7pm Fri, Sat & Sun); Sep–Oct: 10am–6pm Sat & Sun; times vary during school holidays, check website ▪ Adm ▪ www.parcasterix.fr

There's not just the Gaul of Asterix and Obelix to discover here, but six worlds, including ancient Greece and Rome, and all with the charm of Goscinny and Uderzo's beloved comic books. Dozens of attractions include one of Europe's longest roller coasters.

3 Eiffel Tower

A trip to the top is one of the most memorable activities for children in Paris (see pp24–5).

4 Grande Galerie de l'Evolution

The most exciting and imaginatively designed section in the Muséum National d'Histoire Naturelle (see p135) is the Great Gallery of Evolution. Elephants, giraffes and other stuffed animals rise out of a recreated savannah, and a huge whale skeleton hangs from the ceiling, while special displays help tell the story of the development of life on Earth. Nature workshops are also held for children during school holidays.

5 Disneyland® Paris

The French offspring of America's favourite theme park (see p155) is a clone of its parent, and features two parks, including the Walt Disney Studios® complex. There are rides for children of all ages and most adults are equally enchanted.

6 Parc de la Villette

One of the city's top children's attractions (see p156), with activities for all ages. The huge Cité des Sciences et de l'Industrie, a high-tech hands-on science museum, gets star billing, while the Cité des Enfants is a science and nature attraction specifically for younger children. Kids also adore the Argonaute, a real 1950s submarine that voyaged around the world 10 times, the Géode with its IMAX screen and the futuristic outdoor playground.

Parc de la Villette

Jardin d'Acclimatation

MAP A2 ■ Bois de Boulogne, 75016 ■ Open 11am–6pm daily ■ Adm ■ www.jardindacclimatation.fr

This amusement park at the north end of the Bois de Boulogne (see p156) has roller coasters, pony rides and puppet shows. An electric train, "le Petit Train", runs to the park from Porte Maillot.

8 Musée des Arts Forains

Pavillons de Bercy, 53 Ave des Terroirs de France, 75012 ■ Metro Cour Saint-Emilion ■ 01 43 40 16 22 ■ See website for opening dates ■ Adm ■ www.arts-forains.com

A private museum in a former wine warehouse in Bercy Village (see p59). It is a secret wonderland filled with vintage fairground attractions, automata, theatre props, antique merry-go-rounds and a 1920s hall of mirrors. It is open by appointment for guided tours all year round, but visitors are welcome without prior reservations for 10 days over the Christmas and New Year period to try out the traditional fairground games and ride on the carousels.

9 Jardin du Luxembourg

A green oasis in the heart of the Left Bank, this (see p125) is one of the most popular parks in Paris. It has tennis courts, puppet shows, donkey rides and a modern playground (for a fee). But most fun of all is the traditional Parisian pastime of sailing model boats in the octagonal Grand Bassin and riding the 19th-century carousel.

10 Parc des Buttes-Chaumont

The highest in Paris, this park (see p57) is great for a family picnic. For many, this panoramic hilly site is the most pleasant park in the city. Kids enjoy exploring the rugged terrain with its lake, grassy slopes, suspended bridges and waterfalls, as well as pony rides and puppet shows. Le Pavillon du Lac and Rosa Bonheur are perfect spots for drinks.

TOP 10 MERRY-GO-ROUNDS

Carousel by the Eiffel Tower

1 Eiffel Tower
The Parisian icon (see pp24–5) provides a dramatic backdrop to this solar-powered merry-go-round.

2 Jardin du Luxembourg
Children can play the traditional French game of rings on this historic 1879 merry-go-round.

3 Montmartre
At the foot of Sacré-Coeur (see pp26–7), this grand double-decker merry-go-round has gorgeous painted horses and carriages.

4 Parc de la Villette
An airplane, a hot-air balloon and a Tintin-style space rocket join the wooden horses on this two-storey merry-go-round.

5 Jardin d'Acclimatation
A traditional carousel with wooden horses is just one of the collection of merry-go-rounds here.

6 Jardins du Trocadéro
A wonderful hot-air balloon graces this dual-platform merry-go-round (see p142).

7 Hôtel de Ville
Lucky riders jump on whenever this seasonal merry-go-round appears in the heart of the town (see p44).

8 Jardin des Plantes
The curious Dodo Manège (see p138) features extinct animals including horned, giraffe-like sivatherium.

9 Parc Monceau
This charming little carousel is much loved by the local children (see p157).

10 Jardin des Tuileries
Set among the trees, antique wooden horses spin round this enchanting merry-go-round (see p103).

Following pages Interior of the Opéra National de Paris Garnier

🔟 Entertainment Venues

1 Opéra National de Paris Garnier

Going to the opera here (see p104) is not just a night out, but a whole experience. The theatre went back to hosting opera after a spell as a dance-only venue. The building itself is an example of excessive opulence, complete with grand staircase, mirrors and marble – and even an artificial lake deep underground.

Poster for the Folies-Bergère

2 Folies-Bergère

MAP F2 ■ 32 Rue Richer, 75009 ■ 08 92 68 16 50 ■ www. foliesbergere.com

The epitome of Parisian cabaret, the Folies were, for a time, little more than a troupe of high-kicking, bare-breasted dancers. Today, the venue hosts everything from stand-up comedy to pop and rock concerts.

3 Le Lido 2

MAP C2 ■ 116 bis, Ave des Champs-Elysées, 75008 ■ 01 40 76 56 10 ■ www.lido.fr

Le Lido, reopened as Le Lido 2 in 2022, hosts a range of exciting musicals, and stuns visitors with fabulous musicals and cabarets, featuring special effects including aerial ballets. Many regard this dinner-theatre venue as an essential Parisian experience.

4 Le Crazy Horse Paris

MAP C3 ■ 12 Ave George V, 75008 ■ 01 47 23 32 32 ■ www.lecrazyhorseparis.com

More risqué than the other big-name cabaret shows, the Saloon has a reputation for putting on the most professional as well as the sexiest productions. Striptease features, along with glamorous dancing girls and other cabaret acts. The computer-controlled lighting effects are spectacular.

5 Le Cirque d'Hiver

MAP H3 ■ 110 Rue Amelot, 75011 ■ 01 47 00 28 81 ■ www.cirquedhiver.com

Worth visiting for the façade alone, this whimsical, circular listed building, dating from 1852, plays host to the traditional Cirque Bouglione, complete with acts such as trapeze artists, clowns and jugglers.

6 Moulin Rouge

At the home of the Can-Can, Toulouse-Lautrec immortalized the theatre's dancers on canvas during the belle époque and the results are on display in the Musée d'Orsay (see p17). The show (see p148) still

The neon-lit exterior of the Moulin Rouge

has all the razzamatazz that has been dazzling audiences since 1889. The pre-show dinner is optional.

7 Comédie-Française
MAP L1 ▪ 1 Pl Colette, 75001 ▪ 01 44 58 14 00 ▪ www.comedie-francaise.fr

Paris's oldest theatre was founded in 1680 and is still the only one with its own repertory company, staging both classical and modern drama (in French). Commonly known as the Maison de Molière (House of Molière) – an homage to the 17th-century playwright said to be the patron of French actors – it has been based in the current building since 1799.

8 Opéra National de Paris Bastille
MAP H5 ▪ Pl de la Bastille, 75012 ▪ 08 92 89 90 90 (+33 1 71 25 24 23 from abroad) ▪ www.operadeparis.fr

Opened in 1992, this large modern building was heavily criticized, not least for its acoustics and poor facilities. However, this is still the best place to see opera in Paris.

9 Théâtre du Châtelet
MAP N3 ▪ 2 Rue Edouard Colonne, 75001 ▪ 01 40 28 28 40 ▪ www.chatelet.com

Inaugurated in 1862 along with the Théâtre de la Ville opposite it, this was at the time the city's largest concert hall. It has undergone years of extensive renovation. Its broad outreach programme continues to draw new audiences to a varied reperoire of music, dance, theatre and Broadway shows.

10 Théâtre de la Ville
MAP N3 ▪ 2 Pl du Châtelet, 75004 ▪ 01 42 74 22 77 ▪ www.theatredelaville-paris.com

Once known as the Sarah Bernhardt Theatre, after the great Parisian actress (see p160) who performed here and managed the theatre in the 19th century, today it puts on a range of theatre, dance, and classical and world music shows.

TOP 10 JAZZ CLUBS

Performance at New Morning

1 New Morning
MAP F2 ▪ 7–9 Rue des Petites Ecuries
An eclectic mix of music, with jam sessions and impromptu performances.

2 Au Duc des Lombards
MAP N2 ▪ 42 Rue des Lombards
The best overseas jazz artists come here to play with home-grown talent.

3 Baiser Salé
MAP N2 ▪ 58 Rue des Lombards
Jazz, blues and World Music are the mainstays at this tiny cellar club.

4 Caveau des Oubliettes
MAP F5 ▪ 52 Rue Garlande
Jazz in an ex-dungeon, with free jam sessions on Tuesday–Thursday & Sunday.

5 La Bellevilloise
MAP F1 ▪ 19–21 Rue Boyer
An alternative music venue in Belleville, which is a local favourite for live music.

6 Jazz Club Etoile
MAP A2 ▪ 81 Blvd Gouvion-St-Cyr
Features visiting African-American musicians. Jazzy Brunch on Sunday.

7 Sunset-Sunside
MAP N2 ▪ 60 Rue des Lombards
A double serving of late-night jazz: acoustic and modern at street level; electric, fusion and groove in the cellar.

8 La Péniche Marcounet
MAP Q4 ▪ Port des Célestins, Quai de l'Hôtel de ville, 75004
An old barge converted into a live jazz venue. Its Sunday jazz brunch has become very popular.

9 Le Petit Journal St-Michel
MAP M5 ▪ 71 Blvd St-Michel
New Orleans-style swinging jazz in a lively Latin Quarter cellar.

10 Caveau de la Huchette
MAP N4 ▪ 5 Rue de la Huchette
Worth every penny of the entrance fee.

TOP 10 Fine Dining

Elegant interior of Taillevent

1 Le Cinq

The cuisine at the Four Seasons George V hotel is sublime. Christian Le Squer puts a modern spin on traditional French cooking and is known for such signature dishes as spaghetti gratin (with truffle, ham and artichokes). The dining room looking out onto the courtyard is equally impressive (see p117).

2 Jean-François Piège – Le Grand Restaurant

One the most exciting restaurants (see p107) in Paris, mostly thanks to Piège's masterful cooking, which may include dishes such as a tower of spaghetti with belly pork and truffles, and blue lobster in fig leaves. Everything is spot on here, from the cuisine to the striking decor.

3 Le Jules Verne

Now in the hands of Meilleur Ouvrier de France award-winner Frédéric Anton, this restaurant (see p123) on the second floor of the Eiffel Tower has entered the 21st century. It has been revamped with a pared-back decor and there is a suitably luxurious menu, replete with truffles in winter. Service is excellent and the panoramic views are simply breathtaking, but you will need to book in advance.

4 Taillevent

Exquisite haute cuisine in a 19th-century mansion, Taillevent's (see p117) atmospheric oak-panelled dining room is frequented by a mix of businessmen and romantic couples. Dishes such as rex rabbit with Cremona mustard and black radish feature on the seasonal menu and there's an extensive and exceptional wine list. You need to book well ahead to dine here.

5 Septime

Chef Bertrand Grébaut trained with Passard before setting up this Michelin-starred bistro (see p101) serving excellent seasonal dishes. The elegant, minimalistic decor and an open kitchen complement Grébaut's avant-garde cooking. There are set menus at both lunch and dinner.

Stylish bistro Septime

(6) Le Meurice Alain Ducasse

The star chef's interpretation of modern haute cuisine – based on fish, vegetables and grains – is served in this glamorous restaurant (see p107), along with a selection of fine wines.

(7) David Toutain

Having worked with some of the best chefs in Paris, David Toutain has set the bar high, as proved by his restaurant's (see p123) two Michelin stars. On offer are surprising tasting menus which include signature dishes such as white chocolate salsifies and other original touches.

(8) Pierre Gagnaire

Famous French chef Pierre Gagnaire, an advocate of molecular gastronomy, grows his own produce and creates culinary magic at this modern French diner (see p117). Try the foie gras roasted with anchovies which is served with red tuna tartare and tamarillo.

(9) Arpege

Alain Passard's three-Michelin-star restaurant (see p123) is highly regarded in Paris. Dishes, using produce from the biodynamic garden, might include beetroot in a hibiscus-salt crust with bitter orange. Try his superb signature apple tart.

L'Atelier de Joël Robuchon

(10) L'Atelier de Joël Robuchon

Take a seat at the lacquered bar of this two-Michelin-starred restaurant (see p133) to experience France's top chef Joël Robuchon's take on contemporary cuisine. An open kitchen surrounded by 40 seats allows diners to observe while the meticulously crafted dishes are prepared. Signature dishes are the merlan Colbert (fried whiting), and carbonara with Alsatian cream and bacon.

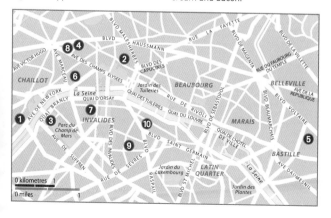

🔟 Cafés and Bars

1 Café de Flore

A hang-out for artists and intellectuals since the 1920s, Café de Flore (see p131) attracted regulars including Salvador Dalí and Albert Camus. During World War II Jean-Paul Sartre and Simone de Beauvoir more or less lived at the Flore. Although its prices have skyrocketed since then, its charming Art Deco decor hasn't changed and it's still a perennial favourite with French filmmakers and literati. Reliable coffee, best enjoyed outside.

Café de Flore

2 Le Progrès

Don't be fooled by the fairly unremarkable exterior of this Parisian bar and café (see p100). Inside, an eclectic mix of locals are always congregating to catch up with friends and people-watch, a drink in hand the meanwhile. Wood panelling and chalkboards give the café a truly authentic, old-world feel.

3 Café Marly

Overlooking the courtyard of the Louvre, this café (see p107) is as sleek as the former palace is royal. From morning coffee to evening wine, Café Marly is the place to rest in between visits to the museum. While it is a far cry from the usual corner café, the experience is justifiably regal thanks to its plush interior and velvet armchairs.

4 Carette

This pavement café (see p101), situated just around the corner from the Jardins du Trocadero, is the perfect setting for lunch. French staples line the menu, and they serve an excellent Sunday brunch. Find a table on the terrace for an exemplary *croque monsieur* or one of the picture-perfect pastries.

5 Café de la Paix

Café de la Paix (see p107) can be found along one of Haussmann's grand boulevards, and has views of the opulent Opéra Garnier. This setting makes it hard to contest the pricier coffee served inside. The café is decked floor to ceiling with decor typical of the Napoleon III style, making it a historic monument. Sip drinks and discuss current affairs like Maupassant or Zola would have in the 19th century.

6 La Closerie des Lilas

The main restaurant here (see p161) is expensive, but the bar is a good spot to soak up the atmosphere of this historic site, where artists and writers such as Georges Braque and Gertrude Stein came to mingle since its founding in 1847. Look out for the famous names of visitors etched on the tables in the bar. The outdoor seating makes for a lovely, leafy setting in summer. The busy brasserie also has live piano music in the evenings and attracts a chic crowd.

7 Les Deux Magots

This café (see p131) was a rival to the neighbouring Flore as a rendezvous for the 20th-century

Pavement tables at Les Deux Magots

intellectual élite. Hemingway, Oscar Wilde, Djuna Barnes, André Breton and Paul Verlaine were all regulars, and Picasso met his muse Dora Maar here in 1937. Like many iconic Parisian cafés, Les Deux Magots is pricey, but the outside tables facing the boulevard and square – ideally experienced with a glass of fizz – are definitely worth the cost.

8 Café de la Mairie

Looking onto the breathtaking St-Sulpice, this classic café *(see p130)* has a fabulous setting reminiscent of a scene from a Parisian film. It is always thrumming with local patrons sipping coffee while they watch the world go by, particularly in summer when additional tables and chairs are set up on the street outside. It's an ideal option for a quick lunch or glass of wine between shopping and sightseeing.

9 La Fontaine de Belleville

The city's best-known roaster *(see p161)* brings artisan drinks to a classic café setting, meaning coffee aficionados can finally revel in a venue with a true Parisian feel. Light breakfasts, delicious desserts and evening cocktails make this place a perfect stop at any time of the day – and lunchtime is the ideal moment for a classic *croque monsieur*. Just up the street from the canal, La Fontaine de Belleville offers a welcome break from the crowds bustling for a waterfront table.

10 Le Relais de la Butte

The terrace in front of this unassuming café *(see p153)*, located high up in Montmartre, is one of Paris's best outdoor theatres. Locals pass the evening watching the sun set over the city as the lights begin to sparkle. The food and drink play second fiddle to the experience of sitting in this little leafy enclave, which in the summer is always busy. Montmartre is laden with watering holes of varying quality, but Le Relais de la Butte is always a sure bet, as long as the weather cooperates.

TOP 10 WINE BARS

La Belle Hortense exterior

1 La Belle Hortense
MAP G4 = 31 Rue Vieille du Temple
= 01 48 04 74 60
A wine bar that doubles as a bookshop.

2 L'Avant Comptoir
MAP M5 = 3 Carrefour de l'Odéon
= 01 44 27 07 97
Jostle around the zinc bar for delicious little bites, and glasses of natural wine.

3 Frenchie Bar à Vins
MAP F3 = 6 Rue du Nil = 01 40 39 96 19
A superb international wine list.

4 Le Barav
MAP R1 = 6 Rue Charles-François Dupuis = 01 48 04 57 59
Well-priced wines in the upper Marais.

5 Le Garde Robe
MAP M2 = 41 Rue de l'Arbre Sec
= 01 49 26 90 60
Cheeses, oysters and charcuterie round out the menu of natural wines here.

6 Septime La Cave
3 Rue Basfroi = 01 43 67 14 87
Quaint wine store of Septime *(see p66)*.

7 Verjus Bar à Vins
MAP E3 = 47 Rue Montpensier
= 01 42 97 54 40
This cosy wine bar specializes in independent French winemakers.

8 Déviant
MAP F2 = 39 Rue des Petites Ecuries
= 01 48 24 66 79
Natural wines pair with small plates here.

9 Le Baron Rouge
An unpretentious, long-time favourite *(see p101)* near the Aligre market that serves fresh oysters when in season.

10 Quedubon
MAP H2 = 22 Rue du Plateau
= 01 42 38 18 65
A list of over 200 natural wines.

Shops and Markets

Galeries Lafayette

1 Galeries Lafayette
MAP E2 ■ 40 Blvd Haussmann, 75009

This expansive store opened in 1894 as a monument to Parisian style, topped by a glorious steel-and-glass dome. Along with designer clothes, there's a fabulous food hall. The seventh floor has great views.

2 Flower and Bird Markets
MAP P4 ■ Pl Louis-Lépine, 75004

Dating from 1808, the colourful Marché aux Fleurs – Reine Elisabeth II (flower market) on the Ile de la Cité is the oldest and one of the largest flower markets in Paris. Its blooms brighten up the area between the stark walls of the Conciergerie and Hôtel Dieu from Monday to Saturday – everything from orchids to orange trees. On Sundays it is joined by the Marché aux Oiseaux (bird market).

3 Printemps
MAP E2 ■ 64 Blvd Haussmann, 75009

One of Paris's top department stores, the iconic Printemps opened in 1864. Its goods range from designer clothing and accessories to mid-range labels and funky fashions, home decor and furniture. The sixth-floor brasserie is crowned with a lovely Art Nouveau stained-glass cupola.

4 Bastille Market
MAP H5 ■ Blvd Richard-Lenoir, 75011

Every Thursday and Sunday morning, this market stretches along the tree-lined boulevard that separates the Marais from the Bastille. Sunday is the best day, when locals come to socialize as well as shop for fish, meat, bread and cheese. Some stalls sell North African and other international food.

5 Place de la Madeleine
This is a gourmand's delight (see p104). Some of the most delectable speciality food shops in Paris are dotted around the edges of this square, including the famous

Fauchon food hall. There's Maille for mustard, Kaspia for caviar, Marquise de Sévigné for chocolates and La Maison de la Truffe (see p106) for truffles. Several elegant *salons de thé* offer a spot to sit and sip too.

6 Merci

Featuring homeware, clothing, furniture and a range of curated design products, Merci (see p98) is a playful alternative to traditional department stores. After a spot of shopping, visit the canteen on the kitchen level or grab a coffee at the charming ground-floor café. It's the place to shop and be seen just north of the Marais.

7 Rue Mouffetard

One of the oldest market streets (see p136) in Paris winds downhill through the Latin Quarter every morning Tuesday to Sunday. Although this formerly cheap and bohemian market has been discovered as a tourist spot, it retains its charm, the narrow streets lined with speciality shops. There are also some good restaurants in the quieter side streets.

8 Le Bon Marché

MAP D5 ■ 22 Rue de Sèvres, 75007

Paris's first department store was founded on the Left Bank in 1852, its structure partially designed by Gustave Eiffel (see p25). Today it's even more hip than its competitors, with an in-store boutique featuring avant-garde fashions. It also has designer clothes,

Le Bon Marché

its own line of menswear as well as the enormous La Grande Epicerie food hall.

Stall at Marché aux Puces de St-Ouen

9 Marché aux Puces de St-Ouen

Porte de Clignancourt, 75018 ■ Metro Porte de Clignancourt

Every Saturday to Monday the largest antiques market in the world is held here. There are actually several markets here: the oldest, Marché Vernaison, is the most charming. Marché Biron offers a wide range of art, fine furniture, interesting jewellery and paintings.

10 Marché d'Aligre

MAP H5 ■ Pl d'Aligre, 75012

Away from the tourist bustle, this market retains its authentic Parisian atmosphere. An indoor hall houses vendors selling cheese, artisan beer, olive oil and charcuterie among other high-quality goods. Outside, inexpensive fruit, vegetables and flowers fill the street-side stands each morning from Tuesday to Sunday.

🔟 Paris for Free

Picturesque Place des Vosges

1 Place des Vosges

Originally named Place Royale, this exceptionally beautiful arcaded square *(see p93)* dating to 1605 is a peaceful area to stroll and sit. The Classical arcades contain many art galleries. At No. 6, the Maison de Victor Hugo is the former dwelling of the famous writer and contains a museum dedicated to his life. The permanent collections are free.

2 Festival de Cinéma en Plein Air

229 Ave Jean Jaurès, 75019 ▪ Metro **Porte de Pantin** ▪ **www.lavillette.com**

Each summer a giant screen is placed in Parc de la Villette *(see p156)*, showing movies (in the original language, with French subtitles) in the open air every evening for a month. The films, which range from classics to the less well-known, are all free. Deckchairs and blankets are available for hire, and many people bring their own picnic to make an evening of it.

3 Musée des Beaux Arts de la Ville de Paris

The grand Neo-Classical Petit Palais *(see p112)* is anything but "little", and is home to this fascinating collection of art and artifacts, including some fine Art Nouveau pieces. There's a charming inner garden with a café too. Check the website for details about occasional free lunchtime concerts held in the auditorium.

4 Free Visits to Museums

On the first Sunday of every month, admission to the permanent collections of most Paris museums, including the Louvre (Oct–Mar), Pompidou Centre, Musée Rodin and Musée d'Orsay, is free to everyone.

5 Hôtel de Ville

Paris's grand city hall *(see p44)* hosts regular excellent, free exhibitions, usually on a Parisian theme; a recent show focused on the Liberation of Paris. Free events often take place on the forecourt, but the wide square is just as fine a place to people-watch on any regular day.

6 Berges de Seine

MAP B4–E4 ▪

The Berges de Seine, the stretch of river that runs between the Musée du Quai Branly – Jacques Chirac and Musée d'Orsay, is an attractive, lively promenade with loads of free activities, such as concerts and workshops, board games, a climbing wall and play spaces for children. There's a riverfront walkway on the Right Bank too.

Berges de Seine

Les Journées du Patrimoine

www.journeesdupatrimoine.
culture.fr

On the third weekend of September, many buildings that are normally off-limits, such as the Elysée Palace, are opened up to the public for free.

8 **Musée d'Art Moderne de la Ville de Paris**

This museum of modern art (see p142), with a forecourt giving onto the Seine, may not rival the Pompidou's collection, but it's free and often offers a calmer atmosphere. Almost all of the major 20th-century artists who worked in France are represented, including Picasso, Braque, Chagall and Modigliani, along with some new modern artists.

9 **Cimetière du Père Lachaise**

It is easy to while away an entire afternoon at Père Lachaise cemetery (see p156), tracking down celebrity graves including those of Oscar Wilde, Colette, Balzac, Edith Piaf, Chopin and Jim Morrison. With its moss-grown tombs and ancient trees, it's also an atmospheric and romantic place for a long stroll.

Grave of Frédéric Chopin, Père Lachaise

10 **Organ and Choir Recitals**
Free organ recitals are given at 5pm on Sundays in the beautiful church of St-Eustache (see p85), which has one of the finest organs in France. La Madeleine (see p46) and Saint-Roch also host free classical music concerts.

TOP 10 BUDGET TIPS

A classic French breakfast

1 Out for breakfast
Having breakfast at a café will cost considerably less than at a hotel.

2 Youth savings
State-run museums, including the Louvre, are free for anyone under 18 and EU citizens under 26.

3 Set-price lunch
Fixed price (prix fixe) lunches are usually good value and almost always cost less than evening meals. They can be a great way of dining at a top restaurant without breaking the bank.

4 Cutting transport costs
Buying a carnet of tickets, a Mobilis or Paris Visite card will save on transport costs (see p165).

5 Lodgings for less
It's almost always cheaper to stay in an apartment, B&B or hostel than at a hotel (see p171).

6 Cut-price entertainment
Half-price same-day theatre and concert tickets are sold at kiosks on Place de la Madeleine.

7 Order a carafe
A carafe of wine is better value than a bottle, and the house wine is generally very good.

8 Museum pass
With so many museums to visit, the Paris Museum Pass offers savings (www.parismuseumpass.com).

9 Sightseeing by bus
The bus is a great way of sightseeing cheaply – for example, number 24 takes a scenic route along the Seine.

10 Cheaper movies
Cinemas in the 5th arrondissement (around the Panthéon) are cheaper than those elsewhere.

🔟 Festivals and Events

Fête de la Musique street performers

1 Street Music
www.fetedelamusique.culture.gouv.fr

Parisians love to celebrate music. The Fête de la Musique, held on the summer equinox, is Paris's largest music festival, when amateur and professional musicians take to the streets. There are performances in Place de la République and concert venues, but the most fun is to be had wandering through neighbourhoods.

2 Garden Magic
www.chateauversailles-spectacles.fr

During summer weekend evenings the gardens of Versailles are home to the Grandes Eaux Nocturnes. Superb illuminations and install-ations, plus a dazzling firework display over the Grand Canal, make this a midsummer night's dream.

3 All That Jazz
www.parisjazzfestival.fr
▪ www.jazzalavillette.com

Paris has a long tradition of jazz, which was introduced to the city in World War I. A summer highlight is the Paris Jazz Festival. The Parc Floral in the Bois de Vincennes (see p156) is the main setting, blending a verdant backdrop with jazz melodies. Jazz à la Villette in September takes place in the Cité de la Musique.

4 Film Screenings
www.feteducinema.com

Cinema is embedded in Paris's culture. The four-day Fête du Cinema, held in early summer, allows film buffs to watch films at cinemas across Paris for just €4. The focus is on niche, independent movies.

5 Cycling Mania
www.letour.fr

Don't miss the Tour de France if you want to understand the French passion for cycling. Held annually since 1903, the world's greatest and most gruelling cycle race approaches Paris after 23 days. On the final laps the riders pass the Louvre, race along the banks of the Seine, hurtle down the Rue de Rivoli and cross the finish line on the Champs-Elysées.

The Tour de France event in Paris

6 City Beach
www.paris.fr

This popular summer event transforms a stretch of the Seine quais and the Canal du l'Ourcq into a mini Cannes, with tons of soft sand, deck chairs, parasols and palm trees.

7 Performing Arts
www.festival-automne.com

From plays and cabarets to music and dance, Paris stages a huge range of shows. For contemporary performing arts, head to the Festival d'Automne à Paris. Founded in 1972, this festival encourages people from all walks of life to performances of dance, music, film and drama.

8 Avant-Garde Art
www.parisinfo.com

A leader in avant-garde art in the early 20th century, Paris continues its cutting-edge artistic legacy with the Nuit Blanche, first held here in 2002. This free all-night arts event in early October provides a fresh perspective on the city, with concerts, plays, installations and illuminations of famous landmarks.

9 Grape Harvest Celebrations
www.fetesdesvendangesde montmartre.com

Paris was once a major wine producer but these days only the vineyards at Montmartre produce wine *(see p149)*, yielding just under a thousand bottles of Clos de Montmartre every year. To celebrate the grape harvest in early October, the Fêtes des Vendanges is held over five days on the Butte Montmartre and neighbouring districts with wine, food stalls, music and street theatre.

10 Foodie Festivals
www.omnivore.com
■ www.paristastefestivals.com

Legendary for its cuisine, Paris is a foodie heaven. Try modern cuisine at Omnivore, a festival in March dedicated to culinary innovation, or savour dishes from leading chefs at Taste of Paris in May.

TOP 10 SPORTS EVENTS

Paris Marathon runners

1 Six Nations Rugby
www.stadefrance.com
The French team plays England, Scotland, Ireland, Wales and Italy.

2 La Verticale de la Tour Eiffel
www.verticaletoureiffel.fr
Race to the top of this iconic monument.

3 Paris Marathon
www.schneiderelectricparis marathon.com
Runners start at the Champs-Elysées and end at Avenue Foch.

4 Football Cup Final
www.stadefrance.com
The biggest event in French football.

5 French Tennis Open
www.rolandgarros.com
This legendary clay-court tournament is part of the prestigious Grand Slam.

6 Top 14 Rugby Final
www.stadefrance.com
Some of the world's finest rugby players take part in the final of the French Rugby league.

7 Prix de Diane Longines
www.evenements.france-galop.com
This upmarket horse race in Chantilly, north of Paris, is named after the mythological goddess Diana.

8 La Parisienne
www.la-parisienne.net
Europe's largest women-only race in aid of breast cancer research.

9 Qatar Prix de l'Arc de Triomphe
www.parislongchamp.com
This world-renowned horse race was first held in 1920

10 Rolex Paris Masters
www.rolexparismasters.com
After the French Open, this is regarded as the country's next major tennis championship.

Paris
Area by Area

A gargoyle stares out over Paris from
Notre-Dame's western façade

Ile de la Cité and Ile St-Louis   **78**

Beaubourg and Les Halles   **84**

Marais and the Bastille   **92**

Tuileries and Opéra Quarters   **102**

Champs-Elysées Quarter   **110**

Invalides and
  Eiffel Tower Quarters   **118**

St-Germain, Latin and
  Luxembourg Quarters   **124**

Jardin des Plantes Quarter   **134**

Chaillot Quarter   **140**

Montmartre and Pigalle   **146**

Greater Paris   **154**

🔟 Ile de la Cité and Ile St-Louis

Paris was born on the Ile de la Cité. The first settlers came to this island on the Seine in 300 BCE and it has been a focus of church and state power over many centuries, home to the great cathedral of Notre-Dame and the Palais de Justice. This tiny land mass is also the geographical heart of the city – all distances from Paris are measured from Point Zéro, just outside Notre-Dame. While the Ile de la Cité bustles with tourists, the smaller Ile St-Louis, linked to its neighbour by a footbridge, has been an exclusive residential enclave since the 17th century. Its main street is lined with shops, galleries and restaurants and is a lovely place for a stroll.

Notre-Dame chimera

ILE DE LA CITÉ AND ILE ST-LOUIS

1 Top 10 Sights
see pp79–81

1 Places to Eat
see p83

1 Shopping
see p82

1 Notre-Dame
See pp20–23.

2 Sainte-Chapelle
See pp36–7.

3 Crypte Archéologique
MAP P4 ■ Pl Jean-Paul II, 75004
■ Open 10am–6pm Tue–Sun ■ Adm
■ www.crypte.paris.fr

Fascinating remnants of early Paris dating back to Gallo-Roman times were discovered in 1965, during an excavation of the square in front of Notre-Dame in order to build an underground car park. The archaeological crypt displays parts of 3rd-century Roman walls, rooms heated by hypocaust, as well as remains of medieval streets and foundations. The scale models showing the evolution of the city from its origins as a Celtic settlement are interesting.

Marché aux Fleurs, Ile de la Cité

4 Marché aux Fleurs – Reine Elizabeth II
MAP N3

One of the last remaining flower markets in the city centre, the beautiful Marché aux Fleurs *(see p70)* is also the oldest, dating from the early 19th century. It is held year-round, Monday to Saturday, in place Louis-Lépine, filling the north side of the Ile de la Cité with dazzling blooms from 8am to 7:30pm. There is also a bird market here on Sundays, which sells some rare species.

5 Conciergerie
MAP N3 ■ 2 Blvd du Palais, 75001 ■ Open 9:30am–6pm daily
■ Adm

This imposing Gothic palace, built by Philippe le Bel (the Fair) in 1301–15, has a rich history. Parts of it were turned into a prison, controlled by the concierge, or keeper of the king's mansion, hence the name. Ravaillac, assassin of Henri IV, was tortured here, but it was during the Revolution that the prison became a place of terror, when many prisoner were held here awaiting execution by guillotine. Today you can see the Salle des Gardes and the magnificent vaulted Salle des Gens d'Armes (Hall of the Men-at-Arms), the Bonbec tower and the prison. The cell where Marie-Antoinette was held, and the history of other famous Revolution prisoners, is on display. Outside, look for the square Tour de l'Horloge, erected in 1370, which houses the city's first public clock, still ticking.

Pont Neuf, Paris's oldest bridge, spanning the Seine

6 Pont Neuf
MAP M3

The name – New Bridge – is somewhat incongruous for the oldest surviving bridge in Paris. Following its completion in 1607, Henri IV christened it by charging across on his steed; the bronze equestrian statue of the king was melted down during the Revolution but replaced in 1818. Decorated with striking carved heads, the bridge was unique for its time in that it had no houses built upon it. It has 12 arches and a span of 275 m (912 ft) extending to both sides of the island.

7 Palais de Justice
MAP M3 ■ 10 Blvd du Palais, 75001 ■ Open 9am–6pm Mon–Fri (ID required)

Stretching across the west end of the Ile de la Cité from north to south, the Palais de Justice, along with the Conciergerie, was once part of the Palais de la Cité, seat of Roman rule and the home of the French kings until 1358. It took its present name during the Revolution – prisoners passed through the Cour du Mai (May Courtyard) on their way to execution during this time – though the Revolutionary Tribunal eventually degenerated during Robespierre's Reign of Terror. In 2018, most of the central law courts that had been housed here moved into new premises in the 17th *arrondissement*.

8 Place Dauphine
MAP M3

In 1607, Henri IV transformed this former royal garden into a triangular square and named it after his son, the Dauphin and future King Louis XIII. Surrounding the square were uniformly built houses of brick and white stone; No. 14 is one of the few

Palais de Justice

THE GUILLOTINE

Dr Joseph Guillotine invented his "humane" beheading machine at his home near the Odéon and it was first used in April 1792. During the Revolution some 2,600 prisoners were executed on the places du Carrousel, de la Concorde, de la Bastille and de la Nation, after awaiting their fate in the Conciergerie prison.

that retains its original features. One side was destroyed to make way for the expansion of the Palais de Justice. Today this quiet spot is a good place to relax over a drink or meal *(see p83)*.

⑨ St-Louis-en-l'Ile

MAP Q5 ■ 19 Rue St-Louis-en-l'Ile, 75004 ■ Open 10am–1pm & 2–7:30pm Tue–Fri, 9:30am–1pm & 2–7:30pm Sat, 9am–1pm & 2–7pm Sun

This Baroque church was designed between 1664 and 1726 by the royal architect Louis Le Vau. The exterior features an iron clock (1741) at the entrance and an iron spire, while the interior, richly decorated with gilding and marble, has a statue of St Louis holding his Crusader's sword.

Square du Vert-Galant

⑩ Square du Vert-Galant

MAP M3

The tranquil western tip of the Ile de la Cité, with its verdant chestnut trees, lies beneath the Pont Neuf – take the steps behind Henri IV's statue. The king had a notoriously amorous nature and the name of this peaceful square recalls his nickname, meaning "old flirt". From here there is a wonderful view of the Louvre *(see pp12–15)* and the Right Bank. It is also the departure point for cruises on the Seine on Les Vedettes du Pont Neuf *(see p171)*.

A DAY ON THE ISLANDS

▶ MORNING

View the exterior of the famous **Notre-Dame** *(see pp20–23)*. This 850-year old cathedral suffered extensive damage in a major fire in 2019. It is now closed for renovations. From here head for the fragrant **Marché aux Fleurs** *(see p79)*. You can buy all kinds of garden accessories, flowers and seeds. Take a coffee break at **Le Flore en l'Ile** *(see p83)*, with its views of the cathedral and the Seine.

The **Crypte Archéologique** *(see p79)* is worth a half-hour visit, before strolling towards **Place Dauphine**. This historic square is the perfect place to relax.

There are plenty of places for lunch, but on a sunny day try **La Rose de France** *(see p83)*, which has terrace seating.

AFTERNOON

Soak up the views of the city from **Pont Neuf** before heading towards the **Conciergerie** *(see p79)*. See Marie-Antoinette's prison cell in this Gothic palace-turned-prison. Next, spend the rest of the afternoon at the ethereal **Sainte-Chapelle** *(see pp36–7)* when the sun beams through the lovely stained-glass windows. From here, start strolling the narrow streets of the beautiful **Ile St-Louis**, which are filled with shops and galleries *(see p82)* selling a wide range of Parisian products.

Wind up with an afternoon treat by visiting **Berthillon** *(see p83)*, considered the best ice cream purveyor in all of France.

See map on pp78–9 ←

Shopping

1 Lafitte
MAP P4 ▪ 8 Rue Jean du Bellay, 75004 ▪ Closed Sun, Mon

Foie gras and other regional products from the southwest await those looking to indulge in French gastronomy.

2 EFFIGYS
MAP Q4 ▪ 37 rue Saint-Louis en l'île, 75004 ▪ Open 11am-7pm daily

A souvenir shop aimed at both adults and children, selling Paris-themed gifts, such as hand-cut jigsaw puzzles, perfumed candles and music boxes.

3 Librairie Ulysse
MAP Q5 ▪ 26 Rue St-Louis-en-l'Ile, 75004 ▪ Closed am & Sun–Mon

Today Paris, tomorrow the world. This eccentric travel bookshop will take you anywhere you want with thousands of titles, antiquarian and new, in French and English – including many on Paris itself.

4 Clair de Rêve
MAP Q5 ▪ 35 Rue St-Louis-en-l'Ile, 75004 ▪ Closed Sun

This boutique sells original puppets, robots and miniature theatres, making it an ideal shop if you're looking for a present with a difference.

5 Laguiole
MAP Q4 ▪ 35 Rue des Deux Ponts, 75004 ▪ Closed Sun (am)

Browse an array of knives and cutlery sets from this iconic cutlery brand, which hails from the Aveyron region of southern France. Look for the famous bee motif on the handles.

6 Pylones
MAP Q5 ▪ 57 Rue St-Louis-en-l'Ile, 75004 ▪ Closed Mon

Rubber and painted metal are used to create the whimsical jewellery and accessories sold here, along with a selection of novelty gifts.

7 Boulangerie Saint Louis
MAP Q5 ▪ 80 Rue St-Louis -en-l'Ile, 75004

One of the few bakeries on the island, this tiny boulangerie has everything classic, ranging from hearty baguette sandwiches to buttery croissants.

8 Maison Moinet
MAP Q5 ▪ 45 Rue St-Louis-en-l'Ile, 75004 ▪ Closed Mon

A family-run confectioner from Vichy, this cute shop sells traditional French sweets and chocolates. It is an enticing treat for all ages.

9 La Ferme Saint-Aubin
MAP Q5 ▪ 76 Rue St-Louis-en-l'Ile, 75004 ▪ Closed Mon (am)

Cheese in all shapes and sizes from across France are sold at this *fromagerie*. An aromatic delight.

10 Carion Minéraux
MAP Q5 ▪ 92 Rue St-Louis-en-l'Ile, 75004 ▪ Closed Sun, Mon

A wealth of meteorites, fossils and minerals. Some are made into imaginative jewellery.

Clair de Rêve boutique

Places to Eat

1 Taverne Henri IV
MAP M3 ▪ 13 Pl du Pont-Neuf, 75001 ▪ 01 43 54 27 90 ▪ Closed Sun, Aug ▪ €

A cosy wine bar with an extensive wine list and simple plates of charcuterie, cheese and snails.

2 Le Sergent Recruteur
MAP Q4 ▪ 41 Rue St-Louis-en-l'Ile, 75004 ▪ 01 85 15 26 80 ▪ Closed Sun, Mon, Tue lunch ▪ €€€

Served in a stylishly refurbished space, the Michelin-starred tasting menus include imaginative modern interpretations of traditional dishes.

3 Les Fous de L'Ile
MAP Q4 ▪ 33 Rue des Deux Ponts, 75004 ▪ 01 43 25 76 67 ▪ €€

This modern Parisian bistro serves typical dishes such as *entrecôte* or steak tartare. It also hosts exhibitions and live music.

4 Le Petit Plateau
MAP G5 ▪ 1 Quai aux Fleurs, 75004 ▪ 01 44 07 61 86 ▪ €

This tearoom is a great lunch spot, serving delicious home-made salads, quiches and cakes.

5 Brasserie de l'Isle St-Louis
MAP P4 ▪ 55 Quai de Bourbon, 75004 ▪ 01 43 54 02 59 ▪ Closed Wed, Aug ▪ €€

Wooden tables and a rustic look complement hearty Alsace fare, such as tripe in Riesling wine. The terrace welcomes alfresco diners in summer.

6 Au Vieux Paris
MAP N4 ▪ 24 rue Chanoinesse, 75004 ▪ 01 40 46 06 81 ▪ Closed Sat lunch ▪ €€

This charming restaurant, with its wisteria-clad façade, is set in one of the oldest buildings on the Ile de la Cité, dating from 1512. The menu features hearty Auvergnat cuisine.

PRICE CATEGORIES

For a three-course meal for one with half a bottle of wine (or equivalent meal), taxes and extra charges

€ under €30 €€ €30–€50 €€€ over €50

---

7 La Rose de France
MAP M3 ▪ 24 Pl Dauphine, 75001 ▪ 01 43 54 10 12 ▪ €€

Dine on French classics on the lovely terrace or in the cosy dining room.

La Rose de France

8 L'Ilot Vache
MAP Q5 ▪ 35 Rue St Louis en l'Ile, 75004 ▪ 01 46 33 55 16 ▪ €€

French classics still have some surprises – duck confit with raspberries, for example – at this tiny, unpretentious eatery. The table displays of flowers are spectacular.

9 Le Flore en l'Ile
MAP P5 ▪ 42 Quai d'Orléans, 75004 ▪ 01 43 29 88 27 ▪ €€

Go for the views as well as the food at this bistro-cum-tearoom, open from breakfast until 2am.

10 Berthillon
MAP G5 ▪ 31 Rue St-Louis-en-l'Ile, 75004 ▪ 01 43 54 31 61 ▪ Closed Mon, Tue, 1 week Feb, 1 week Easter, Aug, late Oct ▪ No credit cards ▪ €

There is always a queue outside this legendary ice cream and sorbet shop and tearoom but it is worth the wait.

See map on pp78–9

🔟 Beaubourg and Les Halles

The small but lively Beaubourg Quarter, brimming with art galleries and cafés, has become a major tourist attraction since the Centre Georges Pompidou opened in 1977. Les Halles was the city's marketplace for 800 years – novelist Emile Zola called it "the belly of Paris". Its glass-roofed pavilions were demolished in 1969 but many of the surrounding bistros and speciality shops are still here.

Fontaine des Innocents

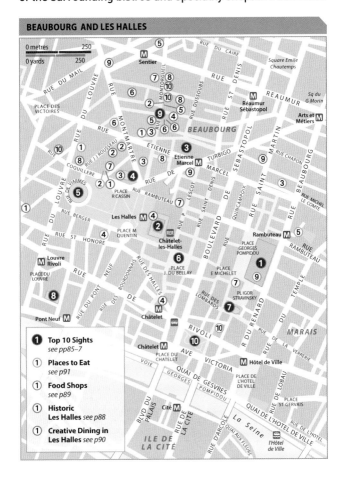

BEAUBOURG AND LES HALLES

	Top 10 Sights
❶	Top 10 Sights *see pp85–7*
①	Places to Eat *see p91*
①	Food Shops *see p89*
①	Historic Les Halles *see p88*
①	Creative Dining in Les Halles *see p90*

1 Centre Georges Pompidou

See pp32–3.

2 Forum des Halles
MAP N2

Ten years after the original market was demolished, the so-called "largest urban hole in Europe" was filled with an underground shopping mall. A recent revamp and a take-over by Westfield have made it more appealing. A huge undulating glass-and-steel roof, dubbed "the Canopy", now crowns the complex, and the surrounding gardens have been relandscaped. Alongside the shops, which include a FNAC bookshop, there are restaurants, cinemas, a conservatoire and a centre for hip-hop (La Place), the first of its kind in France.

3 Tour Jean Sans Peur
MAP N1 ▪ 20 Rue Etienne Marcel, 75002 ▪ 01 40 26 20 28 ▪ Open 1:30–6pm Wed–Sun ▪ Adm

After the Duke of Orléans was assassinated on his orders in 1407, the Duke of Burgundy feared reprisals. To protect himself, he built this 27-m- (88-ft-) tall tower onto his home, the Hôtel de Bourgogne, and moved his bedroom up to the fourth floor (reached by a flight of 140 steps). A remnant of the 15th-century residence, the tower later became a theatre in the 17th to 18th centuries. Today it hosts exhibitions on life in the Middle Ages.

4 St-Eustache
MAP M1 ▪ 2 Impasse St-Eustache, 75001 ▪ Open 10am–6pm Mon–Fri, 10am–7pm Sat & Sun

With its majestic arches and pillars, St-Eustache is one of the most beautiful churches in Paris. Although Gothic in design, it took 105 years to build (1532–1637) and its interior decoration reflects the Renaissance style of this time. The church was modelled on Notre-Dame *(see pp20–23)*, with double side aisles and a ring of side chapels. The stained-glass windows made from sketches by

Chapelle de la Vierge, St-Eustache

Philippe de Champaigne (1631) and the tomb of politician Jean-Baptiste Colbert (1619–83) are the highlights. Don't miss the naïve sculpture in the Chapelle des Pélerins d'Emmaüs, which recalls Les Halles' market days, or the Keith Haring triptych in the Chapelle St-Vincent-de-Paul.

5 Bourse de Commerce – Collection Pinault
MAP M1 ▪ 2 Rue de Viarmes, 75001 ▪ Open Wed–Mon 11am–7pm (Fri till 9pm) ▪ www.pinaultcollection.com

A former grain market and then Commodities Exchange, this impressive circular building, dating from 1767, has been transformed into an exhibition space housing the substantial collection of billionaire businessman François Pinault's contemporary art. As well as an array of changing art exhibitions, there are music concerts, film screenings and conferences.

Façade of the Bourse de Commerce

6 Fontaine des Innocents
MAP N2 ■ Rue St-Denis &
Rue Berger, 75001

The Square des Innocents is a Les
Halles crossroads and a hang-out for
street performers and young people.
It was built atop a cemetery in the
18th century, from which two million
human remains were transferred
to the Catacombs *(see p58)* at
Denfert-Rochereau. The Renaissance
fountain, the last of its era built in
the city, was designed by Pierre
Lescot and carved by sculptor Jean
Goujon in 1547. It originally stood
against a wall on rue St-Denis,
and was moved to the new square,
when the fourth side was added.

7 Eglise St-Merry
MAP P2 ■ 76 Rue de la Verrerie,
75004 ■ Open 3–7pm Mon–Sat (Nov–
Mar: 2–6pm) ■ www.paroisse
saintmerry.fr

Formerly the parish church of the
Lombard moneylenders, St-Merry
was built between 1520 and 1612,
and reflects the Flamboyant Gothic
style. Its name is a corruption of
St-Médéric, who was buried on
this site in the early 8th century.
The bell in the church's northwest
turret, thought to be the oldest in
Paris, dates from 1331. Other highlights include the decorative west
front, the 17th-century organ loft,
beautiful stained glass and carved
wood panelling. There are free
concerts at the weekends.

Stained glass in Eglise St-Merry

GEORGES POMPIDOU

Georges Pompidou (1911–74) had
the unenviable task of following
Général de Gaulle as President of
France, from 1969 until his death.
During his tenure he initiated many
architectural developments in Paris,
including the controversial but
ultimately successful Pompidou
Centre, and the less popular scheme
to demolish the Les Halles market.

8 St-Germain l'Auxerrois
MAP M2 ■ 2 Pl du Louvre,
75001 ■ Open 9am–7pm daily
■ www.saintgermainauxerrois.fr

When the Valois kings moved to the
Louvre *(see p12)* palace in the 14th
century, this became the church of
the royal family. On 24 August 1572,
the tolling of its bell was used as
the signal for the St Bartholomew's
Day Massacre, when thousands of
Huguenots who had come to Paris
for the wedding of Henri of Navarre
to Marguerite of Valois *(see p22)*
were murdered. The church features a range of architectural styles,
from its Flamboyant Gothic façade
to its Renaissance choir. Check
the website for details about the
monthly guided tours.

9 Rue Montorgueil
MAP N1

This bustling market street was
once part of the oldest marketplace
of Paris, the historic Les Halles.
Today, the centrally located and
picturesque street has countless
wine shops, bistros, boutiques,
restaurants and gourmet cheese
and pastry shops, all of which are
a visitor's delight. Many Parisian
chefs frequent the shops along
Rue Montorgueil along with

locals and tourists alike. Its charming and lively cafés are perfect for people-watching after indulging in delicious goods from any of its excellent bakeries.

⑩ Tour St-Jacques

MAP N3 ■ Sq de la Tour St-Jacques, 75004 ■ www.desmotsetdesarts.com

The late Gothic tower, dating from 1523, is all that remains of the church of St-Jacques-la-Boucherie, once the largest medieval church in Paris and a starting point for pilgrims on their journey to Santiago de Compostela in Spain. In the 17th century the mathematician and physicist Blaise Pascal used the tower for barometrical experiments. The church was pulled down after the Revolution. Visitors can take a tour to the top of the tower and visit the gardens (book online).

Tour St-Jacques

A DAY IN LES HALLES

▶ MORNING

Start your day with breakfast at **Le Zimmer Café** *(1 Pl du Châtelet; 01 42 36 74 03; open 7:30am–1am daily)* before exploring the permanent collection of the Musée National d'Art Moderne at the **Centre Georges Pompidou** *(see pp32–3)*. Stop for refreshments at **Le Georges** *(see p91)*, a chic brasserie at the top of the Centre Pompidou, which offers great views along with drinks, snacks or main meals.

On leaving the Centre, turn left into Place Igor Stravinsky to admire the colourful **Stravinsky Fountain** *(see p32)*.

If you have booked ahead, take your seat at Michelin-starred bistro **Benoit** *(see p91)*, whose lunchtime menu is far cheaper than in the evening.

AFTERNOON

Pass the **Fontaine des Innocents** as you head for Les Halles, but first pay a visit to the church of **St-Eustache** *(see p85)*, where the workers of the old Les Halles market worshipped.

Walk under the green canopy over the **Forum des Halles** *(see p85)* and head for charming **Rue Montorgueil** and the little streets surrounding it – there are plenty of food shops and cafés to explore.

Finish the day at the classic brasserie **Au Pied de Cochon** *(see p91)*, which has a smart burgundy-and-cream terrace. It is a great spot for comfort foods such as pork terrine and onion soup *au gratin*.

See map on p84 ←

Historic Les Halles

Sumptuous interior of Au Pied de Cochon

1 Au Pied de Cochon
This 24-hour brasserie *(see p91)* still serves dishes that used to appeal to the earthy tastes of market workers, including the eponymous pigs' trotters.

2 Le Cochon à l'Oreille
MAP F3 ■ 15 Rue Montmartre, 75001

Dating back to the early 20th century, this ornate former working men's café/bar, decorated with historic tiles and murals, has only a small dining room, so book in advance.

3 St-Eustache Sculpture
The lively naïve sculpture by Raymond Mason in the church's Chapelle des Pélerins d'Emmaüs is a tribute to the beloved market. Its colourful figures depict *The Departure of Fruit and Vegetables from the Heart of Paris, 28 February 1969.*

4 Aurouze
MAP F4 ■ 8 Rue des Halles, 75001

This shop is credited with getting rid of Les Halles' most unwelcome inhabitants – rats. The window display is a taxidermy tribute to the once-common vermin.

5 Stöhrer
MAP N1 ■ 51 Rue Montorgueil, 75002

One of Paris's loveliest, old-fashioned patisseries, founded in 1730 by a chef who had worked for Louis XV.

6 Au Rocher de Cancale
MAP N1 ■ 78 Rue Montorgueil, 75002

Once a gathering space for artists and writers during the early 19th century, this place is known for its oysters.

7 La Fresque
MAP N1 ■ 100 Rue Rambuteau, 75001

This wonderful restaurant used to be a fishmonger. Original tiles and a fresco of a fishing scene still decorate the back room.

8 Dehillerin
MAP M1 ■ 18 Rue Coquillière, 75001

Since 1820, everyone from army cooks to gourmet chefs has come here for copper pots, cast-iron pans and cooking utensils.

9 Duthilleul et Minart
MAP P1 ■ 14 Rue de Turbigo, 75001

For more than 100 years this shop has sold French work clothes and uniforms, such as chefs' hats and watchmakers' smocks.

10 A la Cloche des Halles
MAP M1 ■ 28 Rue Coquillière, 75001

This wine bar and restaurant practically chimes with history. The "cloche" is the bronze bell whose peal once signalled the start and end of the market day.

Food Shops

1 **G. Detou**
MAP N1 ▪ 58 Rue Tiquetonne, 75002

The shelves at this chef's paradise are laden with chocolates, teas, artisanal mustards and more.

2 **Mariage Frères**
MAP N1 ▪ 90 Rue Montorgueil, 75002

This elegant and fragrant tea boutique has a dizzying array of teas and teapots.

3 **Charles Chocolatier**
MAP N1 ▪ 15 Rue Montorgueil, 75002

On a cold day, stop in at this family-run chocolate shop for a take-out cup of their luscious hot chocolate; the ice creams in summer are delectable, too.

4 **A la Mère de Famille**
MAP N1 ▪ 82 Rue Montorgueil, 75002

This branch of the oldest confectionary shop in Paris stocks regional French sweets, all in the brand's vintage-inspired packaging.

5 **La Fermette**
MAP N1 ▪ 86 Rue Montorgueil, 75002

The enthusiastic cheesemongers here are ready with tips and tastings to help visitors make the perfect choice from the piles of cheese on display.

6 **Boucherie Roger**
MAP N1 ▪ 62 Rue Montorgueil, 75002

From tender roasted chicken to meat pâté, this place has it all for you. They even prepare their own delicious cuts in-house.

7 **Delitaly**
MAP F3 ▪ 5 Rue des Petits Carreaux, 75002

You'll find fresh and dried pastas, gourmet olive oils, tubs of antipasti and a mouthwatering selection of salami and other cured meats at this Italian deli.

8 **Eric Kayser**
MAP F3 ▪ 16 Rue des Petits Carreaux, 75002

Beyond excellent baguettes, choose from all manner of delicious pastries and other baked goods to stock up on for tea.

9 **Librairie Gourmande**
MAP F3 ▪ 92–96 Rue Montmartre, 75002

This fabulous bookshop has an extensive collection of books on wine and cooking, some in English.

10 **Boulangerie Collet**
MAP N1 ▪ 100 Rue Montorgueil, 75002

Run by the same family for two generations, this boulangerie is known for its *viennoiseries* and light-as-air meringues.

Visitors at Boulangerie Collet

See map on p84

Creative Dining in Les Halles

Stylish interior of Pitanga

1 Pitanga
MAP M1 ■ 11 rue Jean-Jacques Rousseau, 75001 ■ 01 40 28 12 69

Brazilian-born gastro chef Alexandre Furtado's tapas bar serves up delicious modern French-Latin American cuisine.

2 O Château
MAP M1 ■ 68 Rue J J Rousseau, 75001

Get tips for buying wine at O Château. This wine bar runs very popular sessions with English-speaking sommeliers. Consider a tasting dinner in one of their vaulted cellars.

3 Fou de Patisserie
MAP N1 ■ 45 Rue Montorgueil, 75002

This retailer excels in bringing the best pastries from around the city to Les Halles. Sample pastries from some of the most popular chefs such as Pierre Hermé and Cyril Lignac. Here, shoppers can find cakes and other creative products by Paris's biggest names.

4 Champeaux
MAP N1 ■ La Canopée, Forum des Halles, Porte Rambuteau, 75001

Chef Alain Ducasse specializes in French classics and creative cocktails at this ultra-contemporary diner. Good service makes it a perfect stop at any time of the day.

5 Boneshaker Donuts
MAP F3 ■ 77 Rue d'Aboukir, 75002

Away from the traditional pastry shops of Les Halles, Boneshaker produces delicious gourmet, small batch doughnuts.

6 La Cevicheria
MAP F3 ■ 14 Rue Bachaumont, 75002

Try some fresh ceviche – a speciality of raw fish from various Latin American countries. At La Cevicheria it is inspired by its Peruvian version.

7 Lai'Tcha
MAP M1 ■ 7 Rue du Jour, 75002

Michelin-starred chef Adeline Grattard's casual eatery, housed in a handsome modern space, is a dumpling bar in the daytime and a Chinese bistro in the evening – think scallop sticky rice and king crab rolls.

8 Experimental Cocktail Club
MAP F3 ■ 37 Rue St Sauveur, 75002

Although French wine will always reign supreme, the cocktails at this speakeasy-style bar are a welcome addition to the drink options in Les Halles. Dress to impress and prepare to elbow your way to the busy bar.

9 Qasti
MAP G3 ■ 205 rue Saint Martin, 75003 ■ 01 42 76 04 32

Run by Michelin-starred chef Alan Geeam, Qasti is a popular Lebanese restaurant. Choose from mezzes or dishes such as cod in tahini sauce.

10 Grillé
MAP N1 ■ 6 Rue des Petits Carreaux, 75002

A new-generation gourmet kebab spot, Grillé serves delicious high-quality meats and baked-to-order flatbreads.

Places to Eat

1 Madame Rêve

MAP M1 ■ 48 rue du Louvre, 75001 ■ 01 80 40 77 47 ■ €€€

This elegant café-restaurant, with its mahogany furnishings, is set in the city's old post office, newly converted into a chic hotel. A great place for lunch, tea or dinner.

2 Au Pied de Cochon

MAP M1 ■ 6 Rue Coquillière, 75001 ■ 01 40 13 77 00 ■ €€

A Les Halles favourite, this specializes in pork dishes. There are traditional brasserie options too, such as oysters and steak.

3 L'Ambassade d'Auvergne

MAP P1 ■ 22 Rue du Grenier St-Lazare, 75003 ■ 01 42 72 31 22 ■ Closed 2 weeks in Aug ■ €€

With the ambience of a rustic inn, this restaurant transports you to rural Auvergne. Plenty of pork and cabbage dishes, as well as sausage and aligot, are served here.

4 Tour de Montlhéry, Chez Denise

MAP M2 ■ 5 Rue des Prouvaires, 75001 ■ 01 42 36 21 82 ■ Closed Sat, Sun mid-Jul–mid-Aug ■ €€

A Les Halles legend for its huge portions and convivial atmosphere. Book in advance.

5 Le Hangar

MAP G4 ■ 12 Impasse Berthaud, 75003 ■ 01 42 74 55 44 ■ Closed Sun & Mon ■ €€

This small, friendly bistro is no secret to the locals, who keep returning for the fabulous food, including the steak tartare and great desserts such as moelleux au chocolat.

6 Le Tambour

MAP N1 ■ 41 Rue Montmartre, 75002 ■ 01 42 33 06 90 ■ €€

This 24-hour bistro draws a lively crowd with its friendly service and hearty French fare.

PRICE CATEGORIES

For a three-course meal for one with half a bottle of wine (or equivalent meal), taxes and extra charges

€ under €30 **€€** €30–€50 **€€€** over €50

7 Café Beaubourg

MAP P2 ■ 43 Rue St-Merri, 75001 ■ 01 48 87 63 96 ■ €€€

The terrace here overlooks the Pompidou Centre. Steak tartare is a house special.

8 L'Escargot Montorgueil

MAP N1 ■ 38 Rue Montorgueil, 75001 ■ 01 42 36 83 51 ■ €€€

At the heart of Rue Montorgueil, this Parisian institution is known for its signature French dish of snails, after which it is named. Enjoy the view from the terrace.

9 Le Georges

MAP G4 ■ Centre Georges Pompidou, 19 Rue Beaubourg, 75004 ■ 01 44 78 47 99 ■ Closed Tue ■ €€€

Sleek design and a great view make this museum restaurant a superb choice for a glamorous night out.

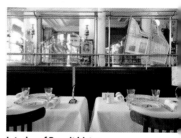

Interior of Benoit bistro

10 Benoit

MAP P1 ■ 20 Rue St-Martin, 75004 ■ 01 42 72 25 76 ■ Closed Aug ■ €€€

Opened in 1912, this Michelin-starred location is, justifiably, the most expensive bistro in Paris. Try the lunchtime menu to keep the cost down.

See map on p84 ←

🔟 Marais and the Bastille

For many, the Marais is one of the most enjoyable quarters of Paris, with chic shops, galleries and dining, as well as fine museums and atmospheric medieval lanes, but the district was little more than a muddy swamp until Henri IV built the Place Royale (now Place des Vosges) in 1605. Following its notoriety as the birthplace of the Revolution, the Bastille district sank into oblivion, until artists and designers arrived in the 1990s. Its streets are now home to the city's liveliest nightspots.

Statue, Musée Carnavalet

MARAIS AND THE BASTILLE

1 Musée Cognacq-Jay
MAP Q3 ■ 8 Rue Elzévir, 75003
■ Open 10am–6pm Tue–Sun
■ www.museecognacqjay.paris.fr

This small but excellent museum illustrates the sophisticated French lifestyle in the so-called Age of Enlightenment, which centred on Paris. The beautiful 18th-century art and furniture on display were once the private collection of Ernest Cognacq and his wife, Marie-Louise Jay, founders of the former Samaritaine department store by Pont Neuf. It is superbly displayed in the Hôtel Donon, an elegant late-16th-century town mansion.

Elegant Place des Vosges

2 Place des Vosges
MAP R3

Paris's oldest square – one of the world's most beautiful – was commissioned by Henri IV. Its 36 houses with red-gold brick and stone façades, slate roofs and dormer windows were laid out with striking symmetry in 1612. While the buildings were originally meant to house silk weavers, the likes of Cardinal Richelieu (1585–1642) and playwright Molière (1622–73) quickly moved in; this remains an upper-class residential address. However, everyone can enjoy a stroll around the area and visit the art galleries under the arcades.

3 Musée Picasso
MAP R2 ■ 5 Rue de Thorigny, 75003 ■ Open 10:30am–6pm Tue–Fri, 9:30am–6pm Sat & Sun ■ Closed 1 Jan, 1 May, 25 Dec ■ Adm (free first Sun of month) ■ www.museepicasso paris.fr

When the Spanish-born artist Pablo Picasso died in 1973, his family donated thousands of his works to the French state in lieu of estate taxes. Thus Paris enjoys the largest collection of Picassos in the world. Housed in the grand Hôtel Salé *(see p96)*, which emerged from extensive renovations in late 2014, the collection *(see p52)* displays the range of his artistic development, from his Blue and Pink periods to Cubism, and reveals his mastery in a wide range of techniques and materials. Larger sculptures are housed in the garden and courtyard of the museum.

1 **Top 10 Sights**
see pp93–5

1 **Places to Eat**
see p101

1 **Fashion and Accessory Shops** see p98

1 **Galleries**
see p97

1 **Fashionable Hang-outs** see p100

1 **Specialist Shops**
see p99

1 **Mansions**
see p96

0 metres 300
0 yards 300

Musée Carnavalet

MAP R3 ■ **16 Rue des Francs Bourgeois, 75003** ■ **Open 10am–6pm Tue–Sun** ■ **Adm** ■ **www.carnavalet. paris.fr**

Devoted to the history of Paris, this fascinating museum sprawls through two mansions, the 16th-century Carnavalet and 17th-century Le Peletier de Saint-Fargeau. The former was the home of Madame de Sévigné, the famous letter-writer, from 1677 to 1696 and a gallery here is devoted to her life. The extensive museum contains period rooms filled with art and portraits, plus Revolutionary artifacts and memorabilia of 18th-century philosophers Rousseau and Voltaire.

Place de la Bastille

MAP H5

Originally, the Bastille was a fortress built by Charles V to defend the eastern edge of the city, but it soon became a jail for political prisoners. Angry citizens, rising up against the excesses of the monarchy, stormed the Bastille on 14 July 1789 *(see p43)* and destroyed this hated symbol of oppression, sparking the French Revolution. In its place is the bronze 52-m- (171-ft-) high Colonne de Juillet (July Column), crowned by the Angel of Liberty, which commemorates those who died in the 1830 and 1848 revolutions. Behind it is the Opéra Bastille, once the largest opera house in the world, which opened on the bicentennial of the Revolution in 1989. In order to divert traffic, certain sections of this busy square have now been pedestrianized.

THE JEWISH QUARTER

The Jewish Quarter, centred on rues des Rosiers and des Écouffes, was established in the 13th century and has attracted immigrants since the Revolution. Many Jews fled here to escape persecution in Eastern Europe, but were arrested during the Nazi Occupation. Since World War II, Sephardic Jews from North Africa have found new homes here.

Passage L'homme

The Passages

MAP H5

The Bastille has been the quarter of working-class artisans and craft guilds since the 17th century and many furniture makers are still located in these small alleyways, called *passages*. Rue du Faubourg St-Antoine is lined with shops selling a striking array of traditional period furniture and modern designs, but don't miss the narrow *passages*, such as Passage L'homme, that run off this and other streets in the Bastille. Many artists and craftspeople have their *ateliers* (workshops) in these atmospheric alleys.

Musée de la Chasse et de la Nature

MAP Q2 ■ **62 Rue des Archives, 75003** ■ **11am–6pm Tue–Sun (till 9:30pm Wed, except Jul & Aug)** ■ **Closed public hols** ■ **Adm** ■ **www. chassenature.org**

Occupying two well-preserved 17th- and 18th-century mansions, this refurbished museum explores the history of hunting, and humanity's relationship with the natural world. Curated to resemble the home of a rich collector, the museum displays tapestries and gilt-framed period paintings alongside taxidermy animals, and fascinating curiosity cabinets. There are surprises in each elegantly organized room, from the astonishing Jan Fabre-designed ceiling of owl feathers to the sleepy fox curled up on a chair.

⑧ Rue de Lappe
MAP H5

Once famous for its 1930s dance halls (bals musettes), rue de Lappe is still the Bastille's after-dark hotspot. This short, narrow street is filled with bars, clubs, restaurants and cafés, and positively throbs with music. Crowds of night-owls trawl the cobblestones looking for action, and spill into the adjoining rue de la Roquette and rue de Charonne, where there are even more trendy bars and restaurants.

⑨ Maison Européenne de la Photographie
MAP Q3 ▪ 5–7 Rue de Fourcy, 75004 ▪ Open 11am–8pm Wed–Fri, 10am–8pm Sat & Sun ▪ Adm ▪ www.mep-fr.org

This excellent gallery showcases contemporary European photography. It is housed in an early-18th-century mansion, Hôtel Hénault de Cantorbre, where a mix of historic features and modern spaces shows off the gallery's permanent collection and changing exhibitions of items from its archives.

⑩ Maison de Victor Hugo
MAP R4 ▪ 6 Pl des Vosges, 75004 ▪ Open 10am–6pm Tue–Sun ▪ Closed public hols ▪ Adm for exhibitions ▪ www.maisons victorhugo.paris.fr

French author Victor Hugo (1802–85) lived on the second floor of the Hôtel de Rohan-Guéménée, the largest house on the place des Vosges, from 1832 to 1848. He wrote most of Les Misérables here (see p48), among other works. In 1903, the house became a museum covering his life.

Busts, Maison de Victor Hugo

See map on pp92–3 ←

A DAY IN THE MARAIS

Marché des Enfants Rouges · Merci · Rue Vieille du Temple · Rue des Francs Bourgeois · L'As du Fallafel · Musée Carnavalet · Rue des Rosiers · Ma Bourgogne · Place des Vosges · Hôtel de Béthune-Sully · Maison de Victor Hugo · Place de la Bastille · Le Train Bleu · 500 mètres (547 yards)

▶ MORNING

Begin at the **Musée Carnavalet** and immerse yourself in the history of Paris. Afterwards, walk to the **Place des Vosges** (see p93): take in the whole square from the fountains in the centre.

Have a coffee at **Ma Bourgogne** (19 Pl des Vosges; 01 42 78 44 64; open 8am–1am daily), right on the square. Head towards **Maison de Victor Hugo**, then go to the south-west corner of the square, through a wooden door to the garden of the **Hôtel de Béthune-Sully** (see p96).

AFTERNOON

If the weather is nice, join the queue at **L'As du Fallafel** (see p101) for a hearty falafel wrap to eat in the nearby square Charles-Victor Langlois. Otherwise, for shelter and a greater choice, head for the lively **Marché des Enfants Rouges** (see p101) and its international food stalls.

Spend a leisurely afternoon exploring the Marais, with its narrow, picturesque streets lined with shops and cafés. Pop into the fashionable boutiques along the **Rue des Francs Bourgeois** and **Rue Vieille du Temple**; bite into a slice of babka in the Jewish Quarter on **Rue des Rosiers**; then explore the ultra-hip Upper Marais, where concept store **Merci** (see p98) holds court.

Walk through **Place de la Bastille** – once the site of the city's dreaded prison – on the way to dinner in style beneath the chandeliers of **Le Train Bleu** (20 Blvd Diderot; 01 43 43 09 06), set inside the Gare de Lyon train station.

Mansions

The beautiful Hôtel de Soubise

1 Hôtel de Soubise
MAP Q2 ■ 60 Rue des Francs Bourgeois, 75003 ■ Open 10am–5:30pm Mon, Wed–Fri, 2–5:30pm Sat & Sun

Along with the adjacent Hôtel de Rohan, this mansion contains the national archives.

2 Hôtel Salé
Built in 1656–9 for Aubert de Fontenay, a salt-tax collector, this mansion is now the home of the Musée Picasso *(see p93)*.

3 Hôtel Guénégaud
MAP P3 ■ 60 Rue des Archives, 75003 ■ Adm

Designed by the architect François Mansart in the mid-17th century, this splendid mansion houses the Musée de la Chasse et de la Nature *(see p94)*.

4 Hôtel de Beauvais
MAP P3 ■ 68 Rue François Miron, 75004 ■ Closed to the public

The young Mozart performed at this 17th-century mansion. Notice the balcony decorated with goats' heads.

5 Hôtel de St-Aignan
MAP P2 ■ 71 Rue du Temple, 75003 ■ Open 11am–6pm Tue–Fri, 10am–7pm Sat & Sun (for permanent exhibits) ■ Adm ■ www.mahj.org

The plain exterior hides an enormous mansion within. It is now the Museum of Jewish Art and History.

6 Hôtel de Coulanges
MAP Q2 ■ 35 Rue des Francs Bourgeois, 75004

This 17th-century mansion was given a fresh makeover by new tenant Collectif Coulanges and is now a concept store and cultural space.

7 Hôtel de Béthune-Sully
MAP R4 ■ 62 Rue St-Antoine, 75004 ■ Closed to the public, except the bookshop (open 1–7pm Tue–Sun) & the gardens

Headquarters of the Centre des Monuments Nationaux, this 17th-century mansion houses a bookshop specializing in French culture and heritage.

8 Hôtel de Lamoignon
MAP Q3 ■ 24 Rue Pavée, 75004 ■ Open 10am–6pm Mon–Sat

This mansion houses the Bibliothèque Historique de la Ville de Paris.

9 Hôtel de Marle
MAP G4 ■ 11 Rue Payenne, 75003 ■ Open 12–6pm Wed–Sun; café: 12–6pm Tue–Sun

The Swedish Institute and its pretty courtyard café are located here.

10 Hôtel de Sens
MAP Q4 ■ 1 Rue Figuier, 75004 ■ Closed to the public, except the library

One of Paris's few medieval mansions. Henri IV's wife Marguerite de Valois *(see p22)* lived here after their divorce. It is now home to a fine arts library.

Medieval façade of Hôtel de Sens

Galleries

1 Galerie Marian Goodman
MAP P2 ■ 79 Rue du Temple, 75003 ■ Open noon–6pm Tue–Sat ■ mariangoodman.com

Housed in a 17th-century mansion, this gallery is a slice of New York style. Artists include Jeff Wall and video-maker Steve McQueen.

2 Galerie Akié Arichi
MAP H5 ■ 26 Rue Keller, 75011 ■ Open 2–7pm Tue–Sat ■ www.akieearichi.com

Exhibitions here cover photography, sculpture and painting, often with an Asian influence.

3 Galerie Alain Gutharc
MAP H4 ■ 7 Rue St-Claude, 75003 ■ Open 11am–7pm Tue–Sat ■ www.alainigutharc.com

Alain Gutharc devotes his space to the work of contemporary French artists.

4 Galerie Daniel Templon
MAP P2 ■ 30 Rue Beaubourg, 75003 ■ Open 10am–7pm Tue–Sat ■ Closed Aug ■ www.templon.com

A favourite among the French contemporary art establishment, this gallery exhibits cutting-edge artists.

5 Galerie Karsten Greve
MAP R2 ■ 5 Rue Debelleyme, 75003 ■ Open 10am–7pm Tue–Sat ■ www.galerie-karsten-greve.com

A leading international gallery with top names in modern and contemporary art and photography.

6 Galerie Patrick Seguin
MAP H4 ■ 5 Rue des Taillandiers, 75011 ■ Open 10am–7pm Mon–Sat ■ www.patrickseguin.com

This gallery features stylish 20th-century furniture and architecture, including works by French architect and designer Jean Prouvé.

7 Galerie Thaddeus Ropac
MAP Q1 ■ 7 Rue Debelleyme, 75003 ■ Open 10am–7pm Tue–Sat ■ www.ropac.net

A major contemporary gallery, Thaddeus Ropac exhibits new and influential international artists.

8 Galerie Sakura
MAP P3 ■ 21 Rue du Bourg Tibourg, 75004 ■ Open noon–8pm Tue–Sat, 2–7pm Sun ■ www.galerie-sakura.com

Pop art and daring works by international photographers are showcased at this offbeat gallery.

Quirky exhibits at Galerie Sakura

9 David Zwirner
MAP Q1 ■ 108 Rue Vieille du Temple, 75003 ■ Open 11am–7pm Tue–Sat ■ www.davidzwirner.com

This powerhouse contemporary art gallery represents a global roster of major artists; the Paris branch is its sixth outpost.

10 Galerie20Vosges
MAP H4 ■ 20 Pl des Vosges 75004 ■ Open 11am–7:30pm Wed–Sun ■ www.galerie20vosges.com

Contemporary artists, painters and sculptors showcase their unique work under the arcades of the regal Place des Vosges.

See map on pp92–3 ←

Fashion and Accessory Shops

Lovely decor at Merci, a fashion-forward concept store

1 Merci
MAP R2 ▪ 111 Blvd Beaumarchais, 75003

This trendy multi-brand store stocks clothes and accessories alongside stylish homewares.

2 Anatomica
MAP P3 ▪ 14 Rue du Bourg Tibourg, 75004

One of the best men's stores in the city, carrying perfectly tailored clothes, and leather shoes from cult brand Alden.

3 Eric Bompard
MAP R3 ▪ 14 Rue de Sévigné, 75004

Everything is soft at this cashmere specialist – sweaters, scarves, gloves and much more.

4 Antoine et Lili
MAP Q2 ▪ 51 Rue des Francs Bourgeois, 75004

Behind the bright pink shopfront, chic and comfortable clothes for women are inspired by Romani and Asian styles, and made using vibrant natural fabrics. They sell children's clothes and home furnishings too.

5 Home Autour du Monde
MAP G4 ▪ 8 Rue des Francs Bourgeois, 75003 ▪ 01 42 77 06 08

French designer Serge Bensimon's popular concept store stocks the brand's classic canvas sneakers in bright colours, limited-edition patterns and pretty Liberty prints for kids as well as adults.

6 Monsieur Paris
MAP R1 ▪ 53 Rue Charlot, 75003

This store sells delicate gold and silver jewellery. Designer Nadia Azoug is often at work in the on-site *atelier*.

7 Sessùn
MAP H5 ▪ 34 Rue de Charonne, 75011

This is the flagship store of the young, French womenswear label, which has chic, edgy clothes and accessories.

8 K. Jacques
MAP Q3 ▪ 16 Rue Pavée, 75004

The classic Saint-Tropez sandal, given iconic status by Brigitte Bardot and never out of fashion, is stocked here, in some 60 styles and colours.

9 Isabel Marant
MAP H5 ▪ 16 Rue de Charonne, 75011

This designer is getting a lot of recognition outside France for her hip but elegant pieces.

10 Bonton
MAP R1 ▪ 5 Blvd des Filles du Calvaire, 75003

A gorgeous store for kids, this has three levels of clothes, accessories, toys and even a vintage photo booth.

Specialist Shops

① Mariage Frères
MAP Q3 ■ 30 Rue du Bourg Tibourg, 75004

This famous tea house was founded in 1854 and sells all kinds of blends, as well as tea-making paraphernalia.

② Jacques Genin
MAP G3 ■ 133 Rue de Turenne, 75003

This trendy chocolatier is adored for his caramels and fruit jellies. He also bakes a fantastic *millefeuille*.

③ La Manufacture de Chocolat
MAP H4 ■ 40 Rue de la Roquette, 75011

The *chocolaterie* of Michelin-starred chef Alain Ducasse smells divine – and has the taste to back it up.

④ Fragonard
MAP Q2 ■ 51 Rue des Francs Bourgeois, 75004

If you can't visit this perfume-maker's factory in the south of France, pick up some soaps and scents in this fragrant boutique.

Soaps and scents at Fragonard

⑤ Liquides Bar à Parfum
MAP G3 ■ 9 Rue Normandie, 75003

Behind its elegant black storefront in the Upper Marais, Liquides carries scents that you won't find anywhere else.

⑥ L'Arbre à Lettres
MAP H5 ■ 62 Rue du Faubourg St-Antoine, 75012

This beautiful bookshop specializes in fine arts, literature and social sciences.

L'Arbre à Lettres

⑦ CSAO
MAP G4 ■ 9 Rue Elzevir, 75003

The Compagnie du Sénégal et de l'Afrique de l'Ouest sells a bright and colourful array of homewares such as woven bags, hand-painted plates and embroidered cushions.

⑧ Papier Tigre
MAP R1 ■ 5 Rue des Filles du Calvaire, 75003

Stylish graphic notebooks, greeting cards and other quirkily designed paper products are on offer at this modern stationery shop.

⑨ Izraël
MAP P3 ■ 30 Rue François Miron, 75004

Also called the "World of Spices", this tiny store is a treasure trove of cheese, wine, rum, honey, mustard and myriad other delights.

⑩ Village Saint Paul
MAP R4 ■ Between Rue St-Paul and Rue des Jardins St-Paul, 75004

An intriguing maze of art galleries, fine antiques and design shops, tucked away behind Eglise St-Paul.

See map on pp92–3

Fashionable Hang-outs

Kitsch decor in Andy Wahloo

the Hôtel de Ville for some above-par brews. It also boasts a shop that stocks coffee beans and unusual jams, as well as a coffee-tasting school.

5 Pop In
MAP H4 ▪ 105 Rue Amelot, 75011
This shabby-chic bar and nightclub has good-value drinks, friendly staff, a cool crowd and funky DJs. It's open seven days a week until late.

6 Café de l'Industrie
MAP H4 ▪ 16 Rue St-Sabin, 75011
A fashionable and sizable café that has three rooms where the walls are lined with paintings and old-fashioned artifacts. The food is inexpensive but pretty good, and the later it gets the better the buzz.

7 Grazie
MAP H4 ▪ 91 Blvd Beaumarchais, 75003 ▪ 01 42 78 11 96
An Italian pizzeria with an industrial loft-style decor, Grazie serves authentic pizzas and classy cocktails, and attracts a hip crowd.

8 Le Panic Room
MAP H4 ▪ 101 Rue Amelot, 75011
Top Parisian DJs set the tone at this quirky bar offering fancy cocktails, a smoking room and cellar dance floor.

9 Le Square Trousseau
MAP H5 ▪ 1 Rue Antoine Vollon, 75012
This charming Bastille district brasserie, with its lovely heated terrace, is something of a media haunt, serving good food from breakfast into the early hours.

10 Le Progrès
MAP R2 ▪ 1 Rue de Bretagne, 75003 ▪ 01 42 72 01 44
The terrace of this corner café in the trendy Upper Marais is the place to be during Paris Fashion Week.

1 Andy Wahloo
MAP Q1 ▪ 69 Rue des Gravilliers, 75003
In one of Henri IV's former mansions, pop art and North African decor form a backdrop for inimitably fashionable soirées.

2 Zéro Zéro
MAP H4 ▪ 89 Rue Amelot, 75011
It doesn't get much cooler than this den-like bar with wood panelling and flowered wallpaper. Though not listed on the menu, cocktails are a speciality.

3 La Perle
MAP Q2 ▪ 78 Rue Vieille du Temple, 75003 ▪ 01 42 72 69 93
This bistro is one of Paris's most famous hang-outs. Its straightforward menu draws a fashionable crowd in the evenings.

4 La Caféothèque de Paris
MAP P4 ▪ 52 Rue de l'Hôtel de Ville, 75004
Coffee enthusiasts congregate at this coffee roaster located behind

Places to Eat

① L'Ambroisie
MAP R3 ▪ 9 Pl des Vosges, 75004 ▪ 01 42 78 51 45 ▪ Closed Sun, Mon ▪ €€€

The finest service matches the finest food and wine. The chocolate tart is out of this world. Reserve ahead.

② Marché des Enfants Rouges
MAP R1 ▪ 39 Rue de Bretagne, 75003 ▪ Closed Mon ▪ €

Food from Morocco to the Caribbean is available at this old covered market. It gets crowded at weekends but is perfect for lunch during the week.

③ Carette
MAP G4 ▪ 25 Pl des Vosges, 75003 ▪ 01 48 87 94 07 ▪ €€

Salads and sandwiches, as well as delicious cakes, feature at this lovely patisserie and tea room on the picturesque Place des Vosges *(see p69)*.

④ Chez Paul
MAP H5 ▪ 13 Rue de Charonne, 75011 ▪ 01 47 00 34 57 ▪ €€

An old-style bistro with a simple but delicious menu and excellent wine list. Reserve your table ahead.

Interior of Chez Paul

PRICE CATEGORIES

For a three-course meal for one with half a bottle of wine (or equivalent meal), taxes and extra charges

€ under €30   €€ €30–€50   €€€ over €50

---

⑤ Le Clown Bar
MAP H4 ▪ 114 Rue Amelot, 75011 ▪ 01 43 55 87 35 ▪ Closed Mon & Tue ▪ €€€

Inventive dishes and natural wines served in a circus-themed, Art Nouveau setting. Try the meaty *pithiviers* (pies).

⑥ Breizh Café
MAP G4 ▪ 109 Rue Vieille du Temple, 75003 ▪ 01 42 72 13 77 ▪ €€

An award-winning crêperie offering savoury and sweet Breton pancakes. The selection of buckwheat galettes includes daily specials.

⑦ Le Baron Rouge
MAP H5 ▪ 1 Rue Théophile Roussel, 75012 ▪ 01 43 43 14 32 ▪ Closed Mon ▪ €

Cold meats, cheeses and oysters are served in an authentic setting next to Marché d'Aligre *(see p71)*.

⑧ Le Temps des Cerises
MAP R4 ▪ 31 Rue de la Cerisaie, 75004 ▪ 01 42 72 08 63 ▪ €€

One of the oldest restaurants in Paris, serving bacon-wrapped scallops, escargot and a selection of desserts.

⑨ Septime
MAP H5 ▪ 80 Rue de Charonne, 75011 ▪ 01 43 67 38 29 ▪ €€€

Dishes such as cress and sorrel risotto and veal tartare are served at this modern restaurant. Book ahead.

⑩ L'As du Fallafel
MAP Q3 ▪ 34 Rue des Rosiers, 75004 ▪ 01 48 87 63 60 ▪ Closed Fri D, Sat ▪ €

This is one of the best falafel joints in the city. The special with aubergine and spicy sauce is a must.

See map on pp92–3 ←

🔟 Tuileries and Opéra Quarters

These two quarters were once the province of the rich and the royal, and there's still an air of luxury about them. Adjoining the lovely Tuileries Gardens is the largest museum in the world, the Louvre, while the grand Opera House gives the second quarter its name. The Place de la Concorde is one of the most historic sites in the city.

**Statue of Medea,
Jardin des Tuileries**

TUILERIES AND OPERA QUARTERS

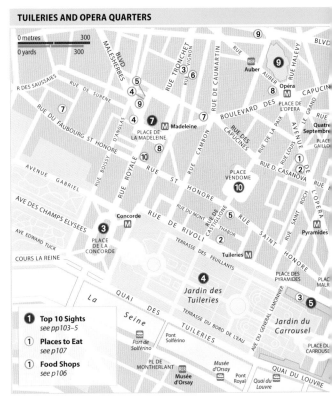

	Top 10 Sights see pp103–5
①	Places to Eat see p107
①	Food Shops see p106

1 Musée du Louvre
See pp12–15.

2 Rue de Rivoli
MAP M2

Commissioned by Napoleon and named for his victory over the Austrians at Rivoli in 1797, this grand street links the Louvre with the Champs-Elysées *(see p111)*. It was intended as a backdrop for his victory marches but was not finished until the 1850s, long after the emperor's death. Along one side, railings replaced the old Tuileries walls, opening up the view, while opposite, Neo-Classical apartments sit atop the long arcades. Since 2020 cars have been banned and bike lanes added, making strolling the street a pleasant experience.

Obelisk in Place de la Concorde

3 Place de la Concorde
MAP D3

This historic octagonal square, covering more than 8 ha (20 acres), was built between 1755 and 1775 as the grand setting for a statue of Louis XV; by 1792 it had become the Place de la Révolution and its central monument was the guillotine. Louis XVI, Marie-Antoinette and more than 1,000 others were executed here *(see p43)*. In 1795, in the spirit of reconciliation, it received its present name. The central obelisk, 23 m (75 ft) tall and covered in hieroglyphics, is from a 3,300-year-old Luxor temple, and was a gift from Egypt, erected in 1833. Two fountains and eight statues represent French cities. On the north side of the square are the Hôtel de la Marine and Hôtel Crillon.

4 Jardin des Tuileries
MAP J2

These gardens *(see p56)* were first laid out as part of the old Tuileries Palace, which was built for Catherine de Médicis in 1564 but burned down in 1871. André Le Nôtre redesigned them into formal French gardens in 1664. At the Louvre end is the Arc de Triomphe du Carrousel, erected by Napoleon in 1808. Also here is the entrance to an underground shopping centre, the Carrousel du Louvre. Nearby, sensuous nude sculptures by Aristide Maillol (1861–1944) adorn the ornamental pools and walkways. At the far end are the Jeu de Paume gallery *(see p53)* and the Musée de l'Orangerie *(see p52)*, famous for its giant canvases of Monet waterlilies.

⑤ Musée des Arts Décoratifs

MAP M2 ■ 107 Rue de Rivoli, 75001 ■ Open 11am–6pm Tue–Sun (to 9pm Thu for temporary exhibitions) ■ Adm ■ www.madparis.fr

This huge collection covers the decorative arts from the Middle Ages to the 20th century. With over 100 rooms, its many highlights include the Medieval and Renaissance galleries, the Art Deco rooms and a superb jewellery collection. There are also displays of fashion, textiles, posters and advertising ephemera showcased in permanent and temporary exhibitions.

⑥ Galerie Vivienne and Galerie Colbert

MAP E3 ■ Galerie Vivienne: 4 Rue des Petits Champs, 75002; Galerie Colbert: 4 Rue Vivienne, 75002 ■ Galerie Vivienne: open 8:30am–8:30pm daily; Galerie Colbert: open 9am–8pm daily

These two 19th-century covered arcades are arguably the most beautiful of the few remaining *passages*. Built to rival each other, both feature frescoed floors and elegant lighting fixtures that enthrall visitors. Today, they house shops, cafés and classes for students at the University of Paris.

⑦ Place de la Madeleine
MAP D3

Surrounded by 52 Corinthian columns, the Classical-style Madeleine church (see p48) commands this elegant square (see p70). On the east side a colourful flower market takes place from Monday to Saturday. Around the square are some of the most upmarket *épiceries* (food stores) and speciality shops in the city.

⑧ Palais-Royal

MAP L1 ■ 8 Rue Montpensier, 75001 ■ Open Oct–Mar: 7am–8:30pm daily (Apr–May: to 10:15pm daily, Jun–Aug: to 11pm daily, Sep: to 9:30pm daily) ■ Public access to gardens & arcades only

In the late 18th century extensive changes were made under the dukes of Orléans. The architect Victor Louis was commissioned to build 60 uniformly styled houses around three sides of the square and the adjacent theatre, which now houses the Comédie-Française (see p65). Today the arcades house specialist shops, galleries and restaurants, and the courtyard and gardens contain modern works of art (see p45).

⑨ Opéra National de Paris Garnier

MAP E2 ■ Pl de l'Opéra, 75009 ■ 01 71 25 24 23 ■ Open 10am–5pm daily for pre-booked, timed slots (to 2:30pm on days of matinee performances and public hols) ■ Adm ■ www.operadeparis.fr

Designed by Charles Garnier for Napoleon III in 1862, Paris's opulent opera house took 13 years to complete. A range of styles from Classical to Baroque incorporates stone friezes and columns, statues

Place Vendôme and Vendôme column

Performance at Opéra Garnier

and a green copper cupola. The ornate interior has a grand staircase, mosaic domed ceiling over the grand foyer and an auditorium with a ceiling by Marc Chagall. There's even an underground lake – the inspiration for Gaston Leroux's *Phantom of the Opera* – sadly closed to visitors (see p64).

⑩ Place Vendôme
MAP E3

Jules Hardouin-Mansart, the architect of Versailles (see p155), designed the façades of this elegant royal square for Louis XIV in 1698. It was originally intended for foreign embassies, but bankers soon moved in and built lavish dwellings. It remains home to jewellers and financiers today. The world-famous Ritz hotel was established here at the turn of the 20th century. The column, topped by a statue of Napoleon, is a replica of the one destroyed by the Commune in 1871.

▶ MORNING

Visiting the **Louvre** (see pp12–15) takes planning, and you should pre-book a timed entry slot online or in person at the ticket desk. Pick up a map as you enter so that you can be sure to see the main highlights. Enjoy a morning coffee in an elegant café in the Richelieu or Denon wings within the museum.

From the Louvre, either take a quick detour to Buren's columns in the **Jardin du Palais-Royal** (see p56) or stroll west along **Rue de Rivoli** (see p103). Turn right onto Rue Rouget de Lisle and walk to the bottom to reach **Da Rosa**, a creative little bistro (19 bis Rue du Mont Thabor; 01 77 37 37 87; open 11am–11:30pm daily).

AFTERNOON

Get some fresh air in the **Jardin des Tuileries** (see p103) then walk down to **Place de la Madeleine** to spend the afternoon browsing in its many gourmet stores, or visit the **Galerie Vivienne** and **Galerie Colbert**. Later, take tea in the café of one of the best shops, **Fauchon** (see p106).

Walk down through **Place de la Concorde** (see p103) towards the 18th-century **Pont de la Concorde** to take in the views over the Seine. Look west towards the **Eiffel Tower** (see pp24–5) to catch a spectacular sunset panorama. Finish the day with a gastronomic dinner at two-Michelin-starred **Le Meurice** (see p107).

See map on pp102–3 →

Food Shops

The chic Pierre Hermé café

1 Pierre Hermé
MAP E3 ■ 39 Ave de l'Opéra, 75002
Follow the rainbow of exquisite macarons in classic and more intriguing flavours at this shop.

2 Cedric Grolet Opéra
MAP E3 ■ 35 Ave de l'Opéra, 75002
Award-winning *pâtissier* Cedric Grolet's stunning cakes and fruit tarts appear as art against the minimalist decor of his shop.

3 Marquise de Sévigné
MAP D3 ■ 16 Rue Tronchet, 75009
Chocolates and *dragées* (sugar-coated almonds) are the speciality at this haven for those with a sweet tooth.

4 Caviar Kaspia
MAP D3 ■ 17 Pl de la Madeleine, 75008
The peak of indulgence. Choose from caviars from around the world, plus smoked eel, salmon and other fishy fare, along with a wide range of vodkas. Try an amazing baked potato with caviar in the upstairs dining room.

5 La Maison de la Truffe
MAP D3 ■ 19 Pl de la Madeleine, 75008
France's finest black truffles are sold here during the winter. Preserved truffles and other delicacies can be savoured in the shop or at home.

6 La Maison du Miel
MAP D3 ■ 24 Rue Vignon, 75009
The "house of honey", family-owned since 1908, is the place to try speciality honeys, to spread on your toast or your body in the form of soaps and oils.

7 La Maison du Chocolat
MAP E3 ■ 8 Blvd de la Madeleine, 75009
A superb chocolate shop, which offers fine chocolates and exquisite patisserie including eclairs, tarts and mouthwatering macarons.

8 Maille
MAP D3 ■ 6 Pl de la Madeleine, 75008
The retail outlet for one of France's finest mustard-makers. Fresh mustard is served in lovely ceramic jars and seasonal limited-edition mustards are also available.

Jar of Maille mustard

9 Lafayette Gourmet
MAP E2 ■ 35 Blvd Haussmann, 75009
Galeries Lafayette's luxurious food hall has an array of breads, pastries, chocolate, wines and other treats, as well as an in-store café and dining counters.

10 Ladurée
MAP D3 ■ 16 Rue Royale, 75008
This splendid *belle époque* tea salon has been serving some of the best macarons in Paris since 1862.

Places to Eat

1 Café Marly
MAP E4 ■ 93 Rue de Rivoli, 75001 ■ 01 49 26 06 60 ■ €€

Set in one of Paris's most enchanting locations, this brasserie *(see p68)* overlooks the glass pyramid of the Louvre. The menu is creative and irresistible.

2 Le Meurice Alain Ducasse
MAP E3 ■ 228 Rue de Rivoli, 75001 ■ 01 44 58 10 55 ■ Closed Sat, Sun, Aug ■ €€€

Try exquisite dishes with pure flavours at Alain Ducasse's splendid two-Michelin-starred venue.

3 Loulou
MAP M2 ■ 107 Rue de Rivoli, 75001 ■ 01 42 60 41 96 ■ €€€

The Musée des Arts Décoratifs' very stylish French-Italian restaurant has beautiful views of the Louvre from its outside *terrasse*.

4 Lucas Carton
MAP D3 ■ 9 Pl de la Madeleine, 75008 ■ 01 42 65 22 90 ■ Closed Sun, Aug, public hols ■ €€€

Chef Hugo Bourny takes the reins at one of Paris's oldest gourmet restaurants. Superb quality food.

5 Café Castiglione
MAP E3 ■ 235 Rue St-Honoré, 75001 ■ 01 42 60 68 22 ■ €€

The burgers at this classic brasserie are so popular that even the style gurus of Fashion Week will indulge.

The elegant Café Castiglione

PRICE CATEGORIES

For a three-course meal for one with half a bottle of wine (or equivalent meal), taxes and extra charges

€ under €30   €€ €30–€50   €€€ over €50

6 Kunitoraya
MAP E3 ■ 1 Rue Villedo, 75001 ■ 01 47 03 33 65 ■ Closed Wed ■ €

There's often a queue at this bustling udon bar serving perfect noodles in a rich broth. A larger sister restaurant is along the road at No. 5.

7 Jean-François Piège – Le Grand Restaurant
MAP D3 ■ 7 Rue Aguesseau, 75008 ■ 01 53 05 00 00 ■ €€€

Located in an elite area, this chic restaurant *(see p66)* with striking and elegant interiors provides modern French cuisine.

8 Café de la Paix
MAP E3 ■ 5 Pl de l'Opéra, 75009 ■ 01 40 07 36 36 ■ €€€

Step back in time at this stunning gourmet restaurant *(see p68)*, which first opened its doors in 1862. The café boasts a beautiful frescoed interior and the menu concentrates on seasonal produce.

9 Restaurant du Palais Royal
MAP E3 ■ 110 Galerie de Valois, 75001 ■ 01 40 20 00 27 ■ Closed Sun, Mon ■ €€€

Contemporary French food is served in the bucolic setting of the Palais-Royal gardens *(see p57)*.

10 Verjus
MAP E3 ■ 52 Rue de Richelieu, 75001 ■ 01 42 97 54 40 ■ Closed Sat, Sun ■ €€€

You need to book in advance for the set six-course gourmet dinner in the intimate dining room, but you can simply turn up to enjoy a lighter bite in the wine bar (47 Rue Montpensier), which doesn't accept bookings.

See map on pp102–3